Casino Games

795
S

Casino Games

Anna Southgate

The Lyons Press
Guilford, Connecticut
An imprint of The Globe Pequot Press

To buy books in quantity for corporate use or incentives, call **(800) 962–0973, ext. 4551,** or e-mail **premiums@GlobePequot.com.**

First Lyons Press edition, 2006

First published in Great Britain in 2006 by Hamlyn, a division of Octopus Publishing Group Ltd 2–4 Heron Quays, London E14 4JP

The Lyons Press is an imprint of The Globe Pequot Press.

10 9 8 7 6 5 4 3 2 1

Printed in Dubai

ISBN 1-59228-908-8

Library of Congress Cataloging-in-Publication Data is available on file.

Card designs based on Waddingtons No. 1 Playing Cards

WADDINGTONS NO.1 PLAYING CARDS
© 2006 Winning Moves UK Ltd
Used with kind permission of Winning Moves

Notes
In this book the gender used in relation to any person is understood to include both genders.

Elements of this book were previously published in *How to Play Poker*, published by Hamlyn.

Contents

Introduction

Introduction

Walk into any casino and you walk into a parallel universe of glitz and glamour. This is a place with a vocabulary and a currency all of its own, where all is luxury and there is no concept of time passing. Join any table and you immediately get a feel for the action, as luck-seeking men and women pit their instincts against the throw of the dice, the turn of a card, or the spin of a wheel.

Never before has the allure of the casino been so great. Since the 1990s, and the building of the first **"supercasinos"** in Las Vegas, casino entertainment has enjoyed an increase on an unprecedented scale and has a well-earned reputation for providing "family fun for all." Las Vegas had 37 million visitors in 2004, no doubt drawn by such spectacles as the Venetian, New York, New York, Luxor, and Bellagio – just a few among the many massive, themed casino complexes that borrow skylines from around the world and boast multi-roomed hotels, golf courses, circus shows, botanical gardens, and ballrooms among their numerous eye-popping attractions.

Of course, Las Vegas is renowned for having the most extravagant casinos in the world and similar resorts are expected to emerge in Britain following current proposals for the **relaxation of the gaming laws**, but they are unlikely to replace the exclusive, club-style casinos that

Las Vegas: America's fastest-growing city

Las Vegas was founded in 1905, when the San Pedro, Los Angeles and Salt Lake Railroad auctioned off 700 lots of land that it had originally purchased to service its railroad construction. The town became a small watering stop with a couple of thousand residents and a few hotels. The building of the Hoover Dam in 1931 brought a second wave of residents, as well as the city's first tourists and businessmen. The same year, gambling became legal in the state of Nevada, while in most of the other states it remained outlawed. By 1940, Las Vegas had a population of 8,500.

The first lavish hotels and casinos opened in the wake of the Second World War, establishing tourism and entertainment as the town's biggest industry. By 1960, the population of Las Vegas had risen to 64,500. The gambling boom took off in the 1960s, buoyed by a wave of corporate investment, and has rarely abated. With an increase of 7 percent a year, the population doubled between 1985 and 1995, rising from 185,000 to 370,000. Estimates for the year 2005 see Las Vegas's population reaching a staggering two million.

The rise of the slot machine

Some 60 percent of a casino's revenue comes from slot machines, certainly in the US. Originally introduced into the casino in the 1950s as an amusement for the wives and girlfriends of the high rollers, they are currently the most popular attraction on the floor. There are more than 165,000 slot machines in Las Vegas alone and part of their appeal lies in the fact that there is no skill required to play them. This, coupled with the fact that there is just the slightest chance that one press of a button could win you a life-changing jackpot, keeps gamblers coming back to the slot machines time and again.

populate much of Europe for now. You will not find the rowdy throng of the craps table dominating here; rather, it is the more gracious air of the roulette and baccarat tables. This is the sophisticated world of James Bond, where entry is usually through membership and is at the discretion of the management.

A brief history

Gambling in one form or another has been evident since the ancient civilizations of Egypt, Greece, and Rome, but it was not until the 17th century that formal venues began to appear specifically for the purpose of gaming. Primarily offering gambling opportunities for the nobility, early casinos opened first in the spa resorts of Europe – such as the Baden-Baden casino in Germany (1748) and the Redoute casino in Belgium (1763) and then, in the early 19th century, along the French Riviera, where gaming houses such as those at Biarritz and Deauville attracted the glitterati of the age. The casino at Monte Carlo, established in 1857 by Prince Charles of Monaco was the first to provide revenue for the state and, as such, is the model on which all modern casinos operate.

Early venues in America, in about 1800, were centered around New Orleans, where professional gamblers, or cardsharps, would make a living working the riverboats that carried passengers up and down the Mississippi. From here, gambling practices moved west with the expansion of the railroads and led directly to the foundation of resorts such as Las Vegas. The 19th century witnessed several changes in attitude towards gambling, and by the early 20th century all gaming in America had been outlawed outright. It was not until the Great Depression in the early years of the 1930s that the state of Nevada saw an opportunity to use gambling to increase revenue, and so laws were relaxed to encourage investors to build casinos in Las Vegas. Despite a disreputable period in the 1950s, when many casinos were associated with corruption and Mafia racketeering, gambling has thrived to become an increasingly respectable and socially acceptable pastime.

Inside the casino

On entering a casino you are most likely to be confronted with all manner of slot machines, ranging from the simplest three-reel fruit machine to video poker. Noisy and vibrant, these machines are among the casino's most popular attractions and there is always a great deal of action to be found here. Beyond them you will discover the main gaming hall filled with tables operated by smart, uniformed croupiers, or dealers. In addition to this, there are usually a number of private rooms, or *salons privées*, in which high rollers can enjoy a serious, high-stake game away from the general hubbub of the main hall.

One of the first questions you face among all of this activity is what to play. Besides the traditional table games, such as blackjack, craps, roulette, and baccarat, there are various other gambling options. These include private-room poker games, lottery-style keno, and a handful of table-game spin-offs, such as mini baccarat and Caribbean stud. While European houses tend to have a lot of action at the roulette and blackjack tables, craps and slot machines are the big draws in the US.

Those who are new to the casino need not feel intimidated by their surroundings. All casinos have useful information on each of the games played and in some houses there is the occasional opportunity to have a lesson in one of the games. You can expect casino staff to be helpful, and a dealer at any given table will help beginners through their game.

Baccarat

Baccarat is probably the most exclusive game in the casino and, as such, it can be intimidating. It is a very simple card game in which two hands are played out – nothing more. There is no skill involved in playing – this is a game of pure chance – and there is no opportunity to lower the house edge, which stands at approximately 1 percent. What draws gamblers to this game are the high stakes involved – baccarat relies on a solid betting strategy and is a game for high rollers.

The dot-com revolution

The World Wide Web has brought an entirely new dimension to gambling and the pace at which virtual casinos are being established is unprecedented: the setting-up costs are a drop in the ocean compared with those of building a new supercasino, and the target audience is ready and waiting.

The first virtual casino – Internet Casinos, Inc. (ICI) was launched in 1995 and, within a year, recorded in the region of 7 million visits per month. Ten years later, the number of gambling-related websites is in the millions. According to Pokerpulse, a company that follows developments in the industry, every 24 hours nearly $180 million are wagered by an estimated 1.8 million players in online poker alone. Gaming consultancy Christiansen Capital forecasts that online gaming revenue will rise to $22.7 billion by 2009, from $8.2 billion in 2004.

House edge

All casino games have what is referred to as a **"house edge."** This is the advantage the casino has over the player and is always expressed as a percentage. In the simplest terms, it is the amount that you can expect to lose, on average, when you play the game. Some games have a higher house edge than others and it is always worth checking the odds before playing a particular game. The house edge derives from the odds offered on the bets you make and guarantees that the casino always wins in the long term. Despite this, it is possible to beat the house edge – making considerable profits – in the short term.

Roulette

Considered the most glamorous game in the casino, roulette involves betting on the outcome of a spin on a wheel. Two versions exist – American and European – with more favorable odds in the latter. Like baccarat, this is a game of chance and there is no opportunity to lower the house edge. Furthermore, the house edge is high in the American game, at 5.6 percent (1.35 in the European version). Because of the high house edge, this is more a game of entertainment than the choice of the seasoned gambler.

Craps

Craps is a great game for action and it is often accompanied by a great deal of shouting and whooping around the table. Part skill, part chance, craps is all about betting on the outcome of a roll of two dice. Rules that seem complicated at first glance are actually very simple, and once the various betting options and craps terminology are clear, this game comes high on the list for entertainment. While some bets carry the highest house edge in the casino, experienced craps players can reduce it to 0.8 percent.

Poker

This is the ultimate game of skill, in which a number of players bet against each other and not the casino. With many variations of the game available, the basic idea is to produce a five-card hand that ranks higher than anyone else's. Gamblers are drawn to the complexity of the game in which there is an obvious element of chance, depending on how the cards are dealt, but also a high level of skill in reading body language and psyching-out opponents. Because the game relies on a series of betting intervals in which players must call, raise, or fold, it is not necessarily the best hand that always wins, but often the best player.

Blackjack

Blackjack is the most played game in casinos today, and it is the first choice for many professional gamblers. It is a one-on-one card game with simple rules, where the object is to beat the dealer. Although there is a reasonable element of chance in this game – there is no way of knowing how the cards will be dealt – there is also an element of skill. By adhering to a well-established basic strategy, it is possible to reduce the house edge to as low as 0.5 percent.

Betting strategies and money management

Gambling is as much about understanding when and how to bet as it is about bluffing an opponent into folding. Knowing how to reduce the house edge through play is only half of the game. In order to leave with more money in your pocket than you arrived with, you need to adopt a betting strategy that works for you and to recognize the principles of managing your bankroll.

Betting systems

Gamblers use a wide variety of betting systems, all of which fall into two main groups: negative progression, where the better bets more when he is losing; and positive progression, where the better bets more when he is winning.

Here are two popular betting systems to illustrate the different strategies:

The Martingale system This method is a very simple negative-progression system where the better doubles his bet every time he loses. It is particularly favored in baccarat, where it works on the principle that the better must eventually have a winning hand. It works like this: if you bet one unit and lose, you double your bet to two units. Lose again, and you double your bet to four units, then eight, and so on. When you do win, because bets are paid at even money, you win back all that you have previously lost, with a profit of your original bet – in this example, one unit. There is a drawback with the Martingale system, however: it is absolutely infallible only if the table at which you are gambling has no betting maximum.

Chips

All casino games are played using colored chips. Each different color chip represents a different monetary value, and each casino uses its own – you cannot take them from one establishment to another. It is possible to change cash for chips on arrival at any particular game: wait until a hand is played out or the dice are rolled before trying to do so. Dealers are not allowed to take money from your hand, so place any cash directly on the table (avoiding any betting spots) and ask for change or chips. The dealer will place the correct amount of chips on the table, which you must take and keep away from the betting areas. All games in the house use the same color-coded chips. The exception to this is roulette in the US, where table-specific chips are used (see page 27). You can change cash for chips at any games' table, but you can change chips back into cash only at the casino's cash "cage," or desk. For the purposes of this book, bets and table limits are discussed as units, where one unit represents one dollar, pound, or euro, depending on where you intend to play.

Managing your bankroll

Knowing how to look after your money is the most critical aspect of gambling, and there are a number of guidelines for keeping you on track:

- Decide on a specific (and realistic) amount of money that you intend to bet with – your bankroll – and do not exceed it.
- Go to the casino with an idea of what you would like to win on any one gambling session.
- Split your bankroll equally between a number of sessions, or days, and be strict about each separate session: if you lose the lot, do not be tempted to spend more; if you win, do not gamble the excess. Send winnings home in the post.

- Be aware of table limits. Realistically, you should play at a table with no fewer than 20 times the minimum bet. For example, if you intend to join a table with a five-unit maximum, you should have at least a 100-unit bankroll.
- Do not deviate from your betting strategy. If you are on a losing streak, ride it – never be tempted to chase it by betting more.
- Never bet if you are tired, depressed or under the influence of drugs or alcohol.
- Take scheduled breaks from the action and recognize when it is time to quit.

The D'Alembert system is a variation on the Martingale system in which you raise your bet by one unit when you lose and reduce the bet by one unit when you win. To be more adventurous, you can vary the sequence and raise or lower by greater amounts with more or fewer wins/losses.

The Paroli system This positive-progression betting system is the exact opposite of the Martingale system – you double your bet when you win rather than when you lose. This is effective when you are on a winning streak – for example, in craps when the shooter has "hot dice," or cannot seem to lose. However, in order to prevent potential heavy losses, you need to have a system in which you let the bet build on only so far before dropping it back to the initial starting bet. For example, you could use a strategy where you bet, then double the bet on each of three successive wins, before reducing the stake to the original amount and starting again.

Table limits

Every table game in the casino will have **"table limits"** – that is a minimum and maximum bet that can be made. You cannot take part in a game without betting the minimum and you cannot exceed the maximum. All table limits are displayed clearly at each table – quite often color-coded to match the chip color of the minimum bet, and it is typical to find a range of tables with different limits for any particular game. In general, tables that are busy tend to be those that allow the lowest stakes – say, a one- to five-unit minimum – while tables that have prohibitively high stakes are often to be found in the private rooms of the casino.

Baccarat

Baccarat

This is an old-world game of elegance and sophistication. A favorite among European royalty, nobility, and rich industrialists for four centuries, baccarat (pronounced bak-ah-rah) has long been associated with high stakes and exclusivity. Even in today's casinos, baccarat tables are customarily sectioned off from the main action, worked by tuxedoed croupiers in plush surroundings, and frequented by the highest rollers of the gambling community.

The name of the game derives from the Italian word *baccara*, meaning **"zero,"** which refers to the point value of all 10s and face cards according to the rules of play.

The game has a rich ancestry, too, with the earliest known version originating in medieval Italy using cards from a Tarot deck. Played in France from the reign of Charles VIII, *c.*1490, the popularity of the game became global with its introduction to French casinos either side of the First World War. It was not long before versions were being played in gambling houses across the globe – most notably in South America, where the game was known as *punto banco* (literally, "player banker"). In fact, it was on watching gamblers play *punto banco* in the Capri Hotel casino in Havana, Cuba, that casino executive Tommy Renzoni persuaded owners of the Dune casino, Las Vegas, to introduce the game to the United States in the late 1950s.

Baccarat basics

In its simplest form, the game of baccarat is played by two betters – a **"banker"** and a **"player"** – who each receive a hand comprising two

Profile of a baccarat player

The average baccarat player is a real chancer. He thrives in the classy, luxuriant atmosphere of the baccarat pit and is lured by the high stakes that dominate the game. He knows he has a good chance of winning – there are only two real decisions to make (which hand to bet on and how much) – and that the payout is good if he gets it right. Most of all, he is attracted to the game because it is one of pure chance – no one hand determines the outcome of the next – and he knows how to ride his luck.

cards. The object of the game is to have a pip count, called a **"point,"** of 9 or lower: the higher hand wins. The remaining betters at the baccarat table bet on the hand they think will win, and/or on whether the two will tie. Although a number of variations of baccarat are played under different names throughout the world (see page 23), these basic rules of the game, and the order of play, are standard.

Table layout

Baccarat is played on a long, hour-glass-shaped, baize-covered table marked with seven betting positions around each short end. There are indents at the center of each long edge so that two dealers and a caller can stand close to the action. Each dealer is responsible for managing the chips and bets at his end of the table, while the caller directs the progress of play. Each position on the table has areas designated for the betters to place bets on the banker or player and/or on a tie. In front of the dealers are numbered boxes – one per better – for commission chips (see page 23).

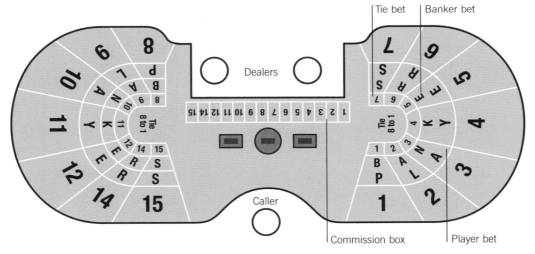

The positions on the baccarat table are numbered 1 to 15, omitting 13 altogether, which is considered unlucky by many.

Baccarat terminology

Banker The better whose role it is to deal the cards to himself and the player. The role passes to the right with each hand.

Caller The casino member who announces the results of each hand.

Dealer Casino staff who take chips and pay out wins to the gamblers.

Natural A point of 8 or 9.

Player The better who plays out the first hand in the game – usually the person with the highest bet on the player hand winning.

Point The pip count of the two cards dealt to each player – always totalling 9 or less.

Shuffle etiquette

The game of baccarat played in most casinos uses six to eight decks of cards, which are shuffled and then placed in a box – called a shoe – on the table. On completion of the shuffle, a marker is inserted between the seventh and eighth card from the bottom to denote the end of the shoe. The hand in play when this card is reached is played out, and the remaining cards discarded. After the shuffle, the caller turns over the top card. The pip value of this card determines how many cards are **"burned"** (discarded) before play starts.

The deal

Baccarat is one of the few games in the casino in which the cards are dealt by one of the betters: starting at position 1 on the table, the shoe passes to each person in turn and he takes on the role of banker. He is responsible for dealing until he loses a hand or no longer wishes to play, and the shoe passes to the next better on the right – that is, counterclockwise around the table. The banker can bet on either hand to win, but must have a minimum bet on the table before taking up the role (see Table limits, page 13).

Once the banker has accepted the shoe (it is not obligatory) and all bets have been made, he deals a card face down to the caller, a card face down to himself, and a second face-down card to each. The banker's cards are placed under one corner of the shoe, while the caller passes his hand to the better with the highest bet on the player hand. This better takes on the role of "player." (If nobody has bet player, the caller takes on the role). After the deal, and any draws that are necessary, the player reveals his cards, followed by the banker.

Card values

The suits of cards in baccarat are irrelevant. All that matters are the card values, which count as follows:
- Aces always count as 1.
- All 10s, Jacks, Queens, Kings count as 0 and totals of 10 made by combining two cards – say, in a hand of 7 and 6 – also count as 0.
- All other cards count as their face value.

In this hand of 7 + 6, the real total is 13 but, since all 10s and totals of 10 count as 0, the baccarat score here is 3.

Naturals

If either the banker or the player has a point of 8 or 9 with his two cards, he scores a **"natural"** and this wins the game immediately. If both players have a natural where one has a point of 8 and the other a point of 9, the higher hand wins. If they both have the same point-value natural, the result is a tie – betters with a stake on either hand retain their bets.

Player's hand – a natural 8
A natural 9 beats a natural 8.
In this case, the banker wins.

Banker's hand – a natural 9

Third-card rules

Should neither party have a natural, the game continues with the player going first, directed by the caller at the table. If he has a point of 6 or 7 the player stands, with the caller announcing "Player stands with 6." If he has a point of 0, 1, 2, 3, 4, or 5, the player must draw another card. The caller announces "Card for the player," and the banker deals a third card, face up this time.

Play passes to the banker, who has to follow strict rules depending on the player's hand. In some situations, the banker is obliged to draw a third card, even if his original hand beats the final hand of the player – although he would not know this until the cards were exposed. Inevitably, this means he can go on to lose the hand depending on what he gains from the draw.

Banker stands on 7

Player's hand   **Banker's hand**

- **The banker stands on a point of 7, regardless of the player's hand.**
  The player has a point of 5 from the deal and must draw. His third card takes his point to 8. The banker has a point of 7 from the deal and must stand. The player wins.

Player stands on 6 or 7

Player's hand   **Banker's hand**

- **If the player did not draw, the banker will stand on 6 or 7 but must draw on 0, 1, 2, 3, 4, or 5.**
  The player has a point of 7 from the deal and so stands. The banker has a point of 2 from the deal and must draw. His third card takes his point to 8. The banker wins.

Banker has 0, 1, or 2 from the deal

Player's hand   **Banker's hand**

- **If the banker has a point of 0, 1, or 2 he must draw.**
  The player has a point of 3 from the deal and must draw. His third card takes his point to 9. The banker has a point of 1 from the deal. His third card takes his point to 8. The player wins.

Banker has 3 from the deal

Player's hand   **Banker's hand**

- **If the banker has a point of 3 he must draw if the player draws 0, 1, 2, 3, 4, 5, 6, 7, or 9, but must stand if the player draws 8.**
  The player has a point of 2 from the deal and must draw. His third card is an 8, taking his point to 0. The banker has a point of 3 from the deal and so must stand. The banker wins.

Banker has 4 from the deal

   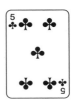

Player's hand   Banker's hand

- If the banker has a point of 4 he must draw if the player draws 2, 3, 4, 5, 6, or 7, but must stand if the player draws 0, 1, 8, or 9.
  The player has a point of 3 from the deal and must draw. His third card is a 4, taking his point to 7. The banker has a point of 4 from the deal so must draw. His third card takes his point to 9. The banker wins.

Banker has 5 from the deal

Player's hand   Banker's hand

- If the banker has a point of 5 he must draw if the player draws 4, 5, 6, or 7, but must stand if the player draws 0, 1, 2, 3, 8, or 9.
  The player has a point of 3 from the deal and must draw. His third card is a 3, taking his point to 6. The banker has a point of 5 from the deal and so must stand. The player wins.

Banker has 6 from the deal

Player's hand   Banker's hand

- If the banker has a point of 6, he must draw if the player draws 6 or 7, but must stand if the player draws 0, 1, 2, 3, 4, 5, 8, or 9.
  The player has a point of 0 from the deal and must draw. His third card is a 7, taking his point to 7. The banker has a point of 6 from the deal and must draw. His third card takes his point to 7. The hands are tied.

Betting in baccarat

Baccarat is one of the easiest casino games to master – it is a game of **pure chance** and there is no skill required from any of the betters. Furthermore, there are just two bets – the player and the banker – and the odds are almost identical. (There is an option to bet on a tie, but this is often made as a side bet in addition to the banker or player bet, and is not particularly recommended – see The odds on winning, below).

However simple the rules, this is not a game for the faint-hearted. Table minimums tend to start high and maximums can reach extravagant levels. Anyone turning up at the baccarat table should have a reasonable bankroll (see page 13) and needs to be aware of popular betting strategies that could work for (and against) him (see page 12).

Strategies

Unlike other table games in the casino – in particular, blackjack (see Chapter 5) – there is no opportunity for lowering the house edge in baccarat (see page 11). The result of one hand has no effect whatsoever on the one that follows, and you cannot influence the outcome in any way. This really is a game of chance. However, a good many high rollers try to detect **"streaks"** in the game and adjust their betting accordingly, using one of several betting strategies (see page 12).

Casinos provide score cards that make it possible to keep track of who wins each hand. This way, betters can easily tell when a game chops back and forth from player to banker or whether play progresses in streaks of runs for either banker or player. Betters base their betting strategies on these observations although, in reality, there is no way to predict the outcome of any one hand.

The odds on winning

Mathematical calculations have shown that the banker has a slight advantage over the player hand, winning 45.8 percent of all hands, while the player wins 44.6 percent (9.6 percent of the hands result in ties). If the house paid even money on all winning bets, this would give the casino a house edge of 1.4 percent on the player hand, but a disadvantage of 1.4 percent on the banker hand. So although all winning hands are paid at even money, the casino charges a 5 percent

Winners and losers

One of the highest rollers to date was Akio Kashiwagi, also known as "the warrior." Betting $200,000 a hand, Kashiwagi famously won more than $6 million playing baccarat in Atlantic City in February 1990. Three months later, having played for almost an entire week, Kashiwagi broke all previous baccarat records with a near $10 million loss.

commission on all winning banker bets to compensate, converting its potential disadvantage into an edge of 1.1 percent. The commission is collected in the form of chips in the commission boxes on the table in front of the dealers and is paid by the players either when they choose to leave the game, or at the end of each shoe. The tie bet is paid at odds of 8 to 1, but since the true odds are closer to 19 to 2, the casino gains a 14 percent edge on a tie.

Baccarat variations

There are slight variations in the way Baccarat is played in casinos in different parts of the world, and these are worth noting if you intend to travel to play the game.

Chemin de fer

An early version of the game, chemin de fer, or "chemmy," is played in France. It takes its name from the French for railway, which is thought to refer to the shoe passing like a train from one banker to the next. It is very like the game described on previous pages, with one major difference: in this game, each banker banks the whole game in turn and must pay out all winning bets. The casino simply takes a 5 percent commission on each banker's winnings. The only other significant difference in this game is that both the player and the banker have the option of drawing or standing on a point of 5.

European baccarat

In this version of the game, the role of banker does not pass from one better to the next, but is taken on by the casino's dealer. The player can choose whether to stand or play on 5 and the banker is not tied to the complicated third-card rules (see page 19) – he can stand or draw as he wishes. Betters still pay 5 percent of their winnings to the casino when betting on the banker hand.

Baccarat en banque

The role of banker does not pass from one better to the next, but is taken on by the casino's dealer. Furthermore, a second player hand is dealt in this game. Betters can bet on either or both of the player hands, but not on the banker. The banker is not tied to the complicated third-card rules and can stand or draw as he wishes.

Mini baccarat

This game is played in the open casino hall on a table much like that for blackjack. Places for seven players are marked, with designated areas for betting on the player, the banker, and/or a tie. A casino dealer deals and plays out both hands, and betters simply decide which hand to bet on and how much to stake. Winning banker hands carry the same 5 percent commission. With lower table minimums and the simplified order of play, this is a less intimidating version of baccarat and is ideal for beginners to the game.

Roulette

Roulette

The true home of roulette is Monte Carlo, for it was here that gambling entrepreneur Francois Blanc and his son, Camille, introduced the wheel to the world-famous casino they established for Charles III, Prince of Monaco, in 1861.

Although early versions of roulette date as far back as ancient Rome, and possibly beyond, the game as we know it has origins in late 18th-century France, from where immigrants took the game to New Orleans in around 1800. The wheel is thought to have been invented by the French mathematician and scientist Blaise Pascal, in researching his theories of perpetual motion. Roulette was played with **two zero** pockets until Louis Blanc (brother of Francois) modified the wheel in 1842, after which **one zero** became the norm in Europe (see page 32). Today, the double-zero game is still played throughout the US and it is the version described on the following pages. The European version is significantly different, and is much more favorable to the player.

Roulette basics

An American roulette wheel has 38 identical pockets, numbered 0, 00 and then 1 to 36. The pockets alternate between red and black as they go around the wheel (the 0 and 00 are colored green) and the numbers, although appearing random, are precisely arranged (see opposite). The wheel rests at one end of a long table on which the betting layout is marked.

The roulette wheel is kept in **perpetual motion**, spinning in an counterclockwise direction, with the croupier spinning it faster once a game is about to begin. He sets a ball rolling along the edge of the wheel, above the numbered pockets, and in the opposite direction to the wheel's spin. As the ball loses momentum, it slows down, bouncing

Roulette terminology

Clocking the wheel Tracking the results of a number of spins to see if any number, or groups of number, are spun more often than others.

Double-zero game The game played in the US, where the roulette wheel has a pocket for both 0 and 00.

En prison An option in the single-zero game, where an even-money bet is held for the next roll rather than lost if the ball lands in the 0 pocket.

Single-zero game The game played in Europe, where the roulette wheel has just one 0 pocket.

Tote board A board found above the roulette table that displays the last 20 or so winning numbers.

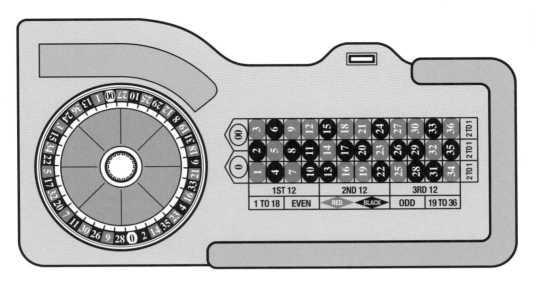

across the wheel a few times before settling in one of the numbered pockets. The aim of the game is to bet on the winning number, and players have many betting options available to them (see pages 28–31). The only caution is that in US roulette all bets are lost when the ball lands on either of the two zeros on the wheel, unless the zero or double-zero is included in the bet.

Roulette chips

Roulette is the only game in the casino to use chips unique to the game. Called **"non-value"** chips, they cannot be used in any other game. Each player – up to six or seven can take part in the action at any one roulette table – buys his own roulette chips at the table. Each one has a different color chip assigned to him and he can decide on its value. For example, a player arriving with 500 casino chips, wanting to make 5-unit bets, will receive 100 roulette chips.

The role of the croupier

Each roulette table in the casino will have a croupier who is responsible for spinning the ball and calling "no more bets" when the ball begins to slow down and bounce across the wheel. Bets made after this call are not valid and chips are returned to the players. The roulette croupier announces the winning number and its color. He then collects all the losing bets and pays the winning bets – outside bets are paid first, then inside bets.

There may be a second croupier at the table, who sorts the chips for winning bets, but it is always the primary croupier who passes winning chips to the players. Once the table is clear, new bets are made and the croupier sends the ball for another spin.

The roulette table: the numbers on the wheel are arranged in such a way that pocket number 1 is opposite pocket number 2, and so on until 35, which is opposite 36. The two zeros are also opposite one another and all pockets are represented on the betting layout.

Placing a bet

When it comes to placing a bet in roulette, players have a considerable choice, with eleven types of bet falling in two different groups – **"inside bets"** and **"outside bets."** Each table has a minimum and a maximum for each type of bet, and you can make as many bets as you like provided you pay at least the minimum on each of the outside bets and you meet or exceed the minimum on any collective inside bets. The odds range from 35 to 1 to even money, with the probability of winning reducing as the payouts increase.

Inside bets

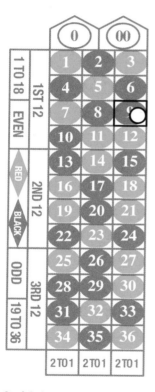

Straight bet
A bet on any single number of the roulette wheel, including the 0 and 00. The chip must be placed squarely inside the box, without touching any of the lines.
Odds: 35 to 1.

Split bet
A bet on any two adjoining numbers on the betting layout. The chip is placed in the line dividing the boxes of the two numbers.
Odds: 17 to 1.

Street bet
A bet on any three numbers in a row on the betting layout. The chip is placed squarely on the line at the edge of the chosen row.
Odds: 11 to 1.

Profile of a roulette player

This is a game of glamour that appeals to the occasional high flyer. He knows the house edge is high and that his chances of making big money in the long run are low, but he cannot resist the thrill of this game of chance and the anticipation of waiting for the ball to land time after time. This gambler is no fool, however, and is certainly shrewd enough not to get carried away with the action at a busy table. He keeps an eye on the tote board and is more than happy to back the odd hunch now and again.

Corner bet
A bet on any four numbers forming a block on the betting layout. The chip is placed at the intersection of the four chosen boxes.
Odds: 8 to 1.

Five-number bet
A bet covering 0, 00, 1, 2, and 3. The chip is placed on the line that separates the 0 and 00 boxes from the 1, 2, 3 row of boxes.
Odds: 6 to 1.

Line bet
A bet on any two "streets" on the betting layout – counting six numbers in total. The chip is placed on the edge of the chosen rows, on the line that intersects them.
Odds: 5 to 1.

Table limits

While table limits might start quite low for minimum bets – between 1 and 5 chips for inside and outside bets, maximums can increase considerably. Maximums for an inside bet might be around 100 chips, while those for outside bets could be as high as 1,000 chips, so there can be much to play for. In some instances, a casino might also suggest raising the table limits for high rollers (see also page 13).

Outside bets

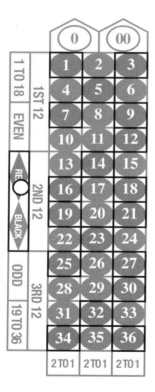  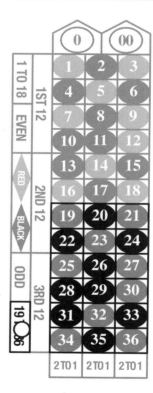

Black/red bet
A bet that the winning number will be black or red. The chip is placed entirely within the relevant box.
Odds: even money.

Odd/even bet
A bet that the winning number will be odd or even. The chip is placed entirely within the relevant box.
Odds: even money.

High/low bet
A bet that the winning number will be either in the low numbers (1 to 18) or the high numbers (19 to 36). The chip is placed entirely within the relevant box.
Odds: even money.

Winners and losers

In April 2004, Englishman Ashley Revell sold all of his possessions and placed the ultimate double-or-nothing bet on a roulette wheel at the Plaza Hotel, Las Vegas. He opted for red to win on his $135,300 bet. The ball came to rest in the pocket of red 7 and the lucky gambler walked away with a cool $270,000 after tipping the croupier $600. When interviewed after the win, Revell claimed that he had intended to bet black until he heard that the viewers watching the event on the Sky One broadcasting channel had voted for him to bet red.

Dozen bet
A bet on the number being in the first twelve (1 to 12), the second twelve (13 to 24), or the third twelve (25 to 36) on the wheel. The chip is placed in the relevant box to the side of the betting layout.
Odds: 2 to 1.

Column bet
A bet on any number within any one of the three vertical columns on the betting layout. The bet does not include the 0 and 00. The chip is placed in the box at the base of the relevant column.
Odds: 2 to 1.

Betting strategy

Like baccarat (see pages 16–23), roulette is essentially a game of chance. The rules are simple to master and there is no skill required from the players. The betting choices may seem complex at first, but are actually straightforward: the narrower the scope of your bet, the higher the odds on winning. A winning bet on a single number promises an attractive 35 to 1 payout – the highest in the casino – but the chances of winning are remote at 37 to 1.

There is no opportunity for lowering the house edge in roulette, which, with an American wheel, is 5.26 percent. (The house edge is significantly lower with a European wheel, see below.) The result of one spin on the wheel bears no relation to the one before it, or to the one that follows, so players cannot influence the flow of the game. Despite that, some players believe that they can detect anomalies, which they can use to their advantage.

The tote board

Most casinos will have a tote board above the roulette table that provides a list of the last 20 winning numbers and their colors. Experienced betters scan the tote board and will bet on numbers that have won twice or more in the last 20 spins, or on sections of the roulette wheel that have a higher percentage of winning numbers than others. Some betters keep their own records of winning numbers – sometimes going back some hundred or so spins – so that they can see the results over a longer period of time. This is known as **"clocking the wheel."** Once a better has spotted a number that wins more often, he might place up to five consecutive bets on that number in the hope that it comes up again.

Playing safe

Above all, roulette is a sociable and entertaining game and, for the amateur gambler, is best kept at that. A good strategy for enjoying the game – and the occasional win – is to manage your funds well (see page 13). Do not be tempted to place a large bet on a hunch; keep the majority of your bets to the even-money side of the betting layout (black or red; odd or even; high or low). And bet sensibly, perhaps increasing your bet by a chip or two when you are winning and reducing it again after a loss (see the Paroli system, page 13).

The European game

Roulette players in Europe have much better prospects all round. Primarily, the wheel has just one zero pocket alongside the 36 black and red slots. This reduces the risk of losing considerably, the house edge being 2.7 percent. Furthermore, the European game employs what is known as the **en-prison rule**. This means that any players with even-money bets when the ball lands on 0 have a choice about how to play on. They can either lose half of the bet there and then, or they can leave the bet where it is to be determined by the next spin. The single-zero wheel and the *en-prison rule* reduce the house advantage on such bets to 1.35 percent.

A form of *en prison*, or **surrender**, does exist in the US – currently only in Atlantic City – where a player with outside bets made when the ball hits 0 or 00 loses only half of his bet. This reduces the house advantage to 2.7 percent.

Another significant difference in Europe is that the game is not played with roulette-specific chips, but with regular casino chips. This can lead to confusion as to who made which bet and how high a stake they made, and so it pays to keep an eye on your chips in case of a dispute. Apart from these differences the game is played in exactly the same way in Europe as in the US. The betting layout is the same, except there is just one zero at the top end, and bets can be made in the same way, with the same odds (although there is no five-number bet in European roulette).

European wheel

The numbers 1 to 36 on the European wheel have a more random arrangement than those on the American wheel.

American wheel

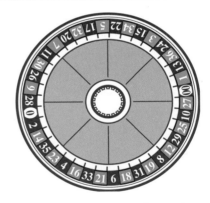

On the American wheel, consecutive numbers appear opposite one another so, for example, 1 is opposite 2, 3 is opposite 4 and so on.

French roulette terms

Many casinos across Europe recognize the French terms for roulette, so you should familiarize yourself with the names of the different bets before playing:

Straight bet *en plein*
Split bet *à cheval*
Street bet *transversale plein*

Corner bet *en carré*
Line bet *transversale simple* or *sixainne*
Black/red bet *noir/rouge*
Odd/even bet *impair/pair*
High/low bet *passé/manque*
Dozen bet *douzaine*
Column bet *colonne*

Craps

Craps

People have been gambling with dice practically since civilization began. Certainly dice forms have been linked to ancient Egypt and it is well known that the ancient Romans made bets on the roll of a die. Today's game of craps can be traced back to medieval England and a game known then as "hazard," in which a main point was established and betters won or lost on the subsequent roll of two dice. This game is believed to have originated in the Middle East and to have been played by the English during the crusades – its name is an anglicized form of the Arabic *az-zahr*, "the die."

Having gained popularity among the English and French nobility during the 17th century, hazard made its way to the US in the early 1800s with the European colonists. It was introduced to New Orleans, where a simplified version of the game, now known as craps, became a regular feature on the Mississippi riverboats. Today's craps layout is the handiwork of one John Winn who, in 1907, introduced the option to bet that the dice would lose. The first layout with the "don't-pass" box marked on it was known as the Philadelphia Layout – after the city of its origin – and it is now the basis of the layout used in casinos across the globe.

Craps basics

Craps is a game played with two dice on a deep-sided, baize-covered table. The name **"craps"** is thought to derive from the English term "crabs" applied to the original losing throws of a 2, 3, or 12. These remain losing throws in today's game. Any number of players can take part, each of them betting individually against the house and not each

Profile of a craps player

Your regular craps player is drawn to the, at times ecstatic, noise and chaos of the craps table. He loves to squeeze in beside other players, getting in on the real action in the casino. There is nothing to beat the thrill of rolling to win and he knows how to beat down the house edge. He might shout and whoop with the others, but he never loses his cool; he knows which bets are the best and he is not going to let anyone persuade him otherwise.

other. Every player has the opportunity to be the **"shooter"** – that is, the person throwing the dice – with play passing to the left. A new shooter chooses one pair of dice from a selection of three before making his first, and subsequent, throws. With the exception of his first roll of the dice – the **"come-out"** roll – each shooter's turn ends as soon as he throws a seven. On the surface of the table is the betting layout, with specific areas for placing more than 30 different bets, some with more favorable odds than others (see pages 41–47). All players place bets on the likely outcome of each throw before it is made, and can bet for or against the "shooter."

Table layout

The craps table is basically a long, rectangular, baize-covered table with deep sides, marked up with the various bets available to players. The betting layout looks complicated, but the majority of the bets are marked on twice, enabling players to stand at either end of the table. There are typically three dealers at work on the craps table. Two of them handle the bets made and the payout from each throw of the dice. The other is known as the **"stickman,"** who handles the dice and controls the speed of the game. The table is also overseen by a boxman, who approves bets and payouts, and settles any disputes.

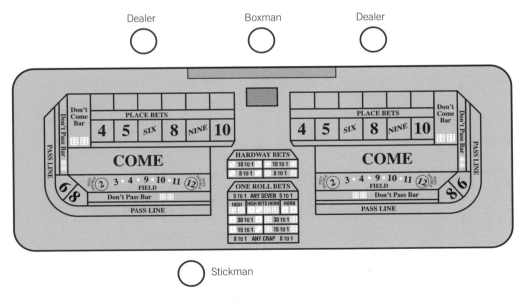

Each shooter must roll the dice the full length of the table, and they must bounce off the end wall before landing to be considered valid.

The "come-out" roll

A player's first throw is called the **"come-out"** roll, in which he must establish his **"point."** In order to do this, the combined values of his two dice must total 4, 5, 6, 8, 9, or 10. A puck is placed on the corresponding number of the betting layout. The shooter now has to roll that same "point" again before rolling a 7.

Players, including the shooter, bet on the outcome of the come-out roll. Placing a bet on the **"pass"** line means that you expect the shooter to be successful in rolling his point again before rolling a 7. This is described as "betting on the dos," or "betting right." Placing a bet on the **"don't-pass"** line means that you don't expect the shooter to throw a 7 before throwing his point. This is referred to as "betting on the don'ts," or "betting wrong."

If the shooter throws a 7 or 11 on the come-out roll, there is an automatic win for everyone who placed a bet on the pass line. Those with bets on the don't-pass line lose. If, however, the shooter throws a 2, 3, or 12 – known collectively as **"craps"** – on the come-out roll, everyone who placed a bet on the pass line loses. Those with bets on the don't-pass line win on a 2 or 3, and tie on a 12.

Once the shooter establishes a point – say 5 – he can throw again to roll another 5 before throwing a 7. Any other roll is a **"waiting"** number and the shooter simply throws again. If he throws the 5 first, the pass-line bet wins, bets are settled, and the shooter throws again to establish another point. He must throw this again, and so on, until he "sevens out" by throwing the 7, after which play passes to the left.

Craps terminology

Boxman The casino representative who sits at the center of one side of the table and supervises the game.

Cocked dice A situation where, after a throw, one or both dice lands so that it is not lying flat on the table. In such a situation, the stickman decides which number it shows (see Craps etiquette).

Come-out roll The first roll of the dice by a new shooter, determining the shooter's point.

Crap out To throw a 2, 3, or 12 on the come-out roll.

Craps Any dice roll that shows a 2, 3, or 12.

Do bet Any bet that favors the shooter over the house. Also known as right bet.

Don't bet Any bet that favors the house over the shooter. Also known as wrong bet.

Natural A throw of 7 or 11 on the come-out roll.

Point A throw of 4, 5, 6, 8, 9, or 10 by the shooter on the come-out roll and which he must then throw a second time before throwing a 7.

Seven out The point at which a shooter loses by throwing a 7 before repeating his point.

Shooter The player whose turn it is to roll the dice.

Stickman The dealer whose job it is to call out the rolls, take proposition bets, and to move the dice around the table using a stick.

Come-out roll summary

- **If the shooter throws a 7 or 11**, all pass-line betters win, all don't-pass-line betters lose; the shooter throws for another come-out roll.

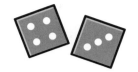

- **If the shooter throws a 2, 3, or 12 (craps)**, all pass-line betters lose, don't-pass-line betters win on 2 or 3 and tie on 12; the shooter throws for another come-out roll.

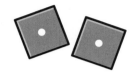

- **If the shooter throws a 4, 5, 6, 8, 9, or 10, his "point" is established**. All line bets stay where they are and players can now place additional bets (see pages 41–47). The shooter continues to roll until he throws a 7.

Craps etiquette

Players should observe the following formalities when playing craps:
- Dealers are not allowed to take money or chips out of your hand or to place money or chips in your hand. If you need to change cash, place certain bets, or take winnings, all will be carried out by placing chips or money on the table first.
- Do not leave winnings on the betting layout, unless you specifically intend to bet with them.
- The stickman and the shooter are the only two people at the table who handle the dice.
- The shooter must roll the dice the full length of the table, bouncing them off the end wall.
- Dice that leave the table, land on betting chips, or in the dice boat are considered invalid and the shooter must roll again.
- A dice that falls cocked is left in play, with the stickman calling the number it counts as.
- All hands should be kept clear of the craps table: it is considered bad luck for the shooter if the dice hits anyone's hands.
- Players are not allowed to place any bets above the come line. This means that dealers move all come-line bets and don't-come bets to the place-bet boxes; place all odds bets on come bets and don't-come bets; and place all place and buy bets.
- The stickman places all proposition bets on behalf of players.

Chances of throwing each number

Point

The most likely number to come up is a 7, which has a one in six chance of being rolled. This is followed by either 6 or 8, then 5 or 9, then 4 or 10, then 3 or 11, and finally 2 and 12, each of which have only a 1 in 35 chance of being rolled.

2

3

4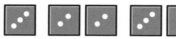

5

6

7

8

9

10

11

12

Betting options

Once a shooter's point is established, the game opens up and additional bets can be placed. Successful play is all in the betting, since each roll of the dice is primarily down to chance and, although it is clear from the table layout that all manner of bets can be made, some of them are more advantageous to players than others. The reason for this is that each roll of the dice pays out at **different odds**, depending on the likelihood of any given number being thrown.

Each roll depends on the outcome of two dice and it is possible to work out how many times a specific number is likely to come up. There are 36 possible combinations in all and the casino offers different odds on each number, depending on the kind of bet being made. By analyzing the payouts of each different bet an experienced player can stake money only on those bets that give the house the least edge (see each individual bet).

Free odds

This is a betting position that is not marked on the betting layout, but is considered one of the most favorable bets for the "do" betters. Once a point has been established, you can place a free-odds bet on the table behind your existing pass-line bet, betting that the point will be thrown before a 7. A winning pass-line bet already carries a reasonably low house edge of 1.41 percent, and you can reduce this substantially with a winning free-odds bet because all free-odds bets pay out at the true odds of the point being thrown – that is with no house edge. A single free-odds bet – that is a bet of the same value as the pass-line bet – can reduce the house edge to as little as 0.85 percent. Some casinos allow you to bet double the value of a pass-line bet, which reduces the house edge even further. While you cannot remove a pass-line bet once you have made it, you can place and remove free-odds bets at will throughout the game. It is worth noting that, while it is also possible to place a free-odds bet when backing the don't-betters, this is not advisable, as the odds are reversed and you need to bet more chips than you stand to win.

Payout on free odds

The true odds of throwing a 6 or 8 are 6 to 5 because there are six chances of rolling a 7 as opposed to five chances of rolling a 6 or 8. Therefore, a 5-chip free-odds bet on a 6 or 8 will win 6 chips. A 6-chip bet on a 5 or 9 will win 9 chips (odds of 3 to 2) and a 5-chip bet on a 4 or 10 will win 10 chips (odds of 2 to 1). You should note that most casinos are unlikely to deal in chips with less than a 1-unit value, so it is sensible to place a 6-chip bet on a 5 or 9. (A 5-chip bet results in a 7.5-chip win, which the casino will round down to 7.)

Come-line bets

This is another bet available to the do betters and it works in a similar way to the pass-line bet. Following the come-out roll, your pass-line bet stays where it is, and you place an additional bet on the come line. The next roll of the dice is treated like a come-out roll for this new come-line bet alone – that is, it works independently of the pass-line bet:

- If the shooter throws a 7 or 11, your come-line bet wins, with an even-money payout.

- If he throws a 2, 3, or 12, the come-line bet loses, and the bet is removed.

- If the shooter throws his point – say 8 – your come-line bet is moved to the "place-bet" box for the point 8.

- If he throws any other point, 4, 5, 6, 9, or 10, your come-line bet is moved to the corresponding place-bet box for that point.

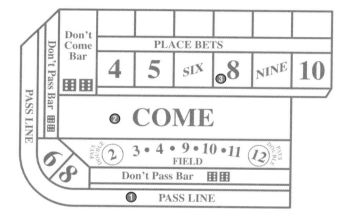

A come-line bet (2) is placed following a come-out roll, and is independent of the pass-line bet (1). Should the shooter's point be repeated, or if he throws a different point on the next roll, the come-line bet is moved to the relevant place-bet box (3).

In the case of the last two scenarios, the come-line bet is now resolved only when the point in question or a 7 is rolled, with a win or a loss, respectively, and where a win receives an even-money payout. Once your come-line bet has either won or lost, or been moved to a place-bet box, you can place another one and so on, giving you bets on several outcomes at once.

Your pass-line bet is still in action when you make a come-line bet. This means that, while you may win the come-line bet on a throw of 7, you would lose on the pass-line bet. The same is true for multiple come bets. If the shooter rolls a 7 on your second come-line bet, and you already have a come bet in a place-bet box, the latter loses along with the pass-line bet, while the former wins.

Come-line summary

To summarize, consider the following scenario: the shooter throws an 8 on his come-out roll, establishing his point. He needs to throw an 8 again, before a 7, in order to win the pass-line bet. You have a pass-line bet on the 8 and place a bet on the come line.

Example of a come-line betting scenario

- **If the shooter throws a 7**, your come-line bet wins, but the pass-line bet loses.

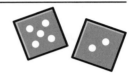

- **If the shooter throws an 11**, your come-line bet wins, and the pass-line bet remains intact.

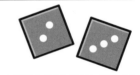

- **If the shooter throws a 2, 3, or 12**, your come-line bet loses, and the pass-line bet remains intact.

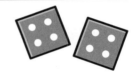

- **If the shooter throws his point** – an 8 – your pass-line bet wins, and the come-line bet is moved to the place-bet box of the 8. This bet is now resolved only when either another 8 is thrown, in which case it wins, or a 7, in which case it loses.

- **If the shooter throws a different point** – 4, 5, 6, 9, or 10 – your pass-line bet remains, and the come-line bet is moved to the place-bet box for that number. This bet is now resolved only when either that number is thrown (to win) or a 7 is thrown (to lose).

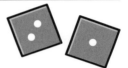

- If, when your first come-line bet is moved to a place-bet box, you place another come-line bet, both the original come bet and the pass-line bet lose if the shooter's next throw is a 7, but the second come-line bet wins.

By placing a come-line bet, or a series of them, you increase the number of outcomes that might bring you a win during the game, particularly if the shooter is on a winning streak. Furthermore, you are allowed to place odds bets on the come-line bet, just as you can with a pass-line bet, and this can significantly increase your winnings. As with free odds, you can place and remove these odds bets at will during play. What you need to remember, however, is that once a come-line bet has been placed, the next throw counts as a come-out roll (for that bet only).

Betting with the don'ts

While the majority of players will bet with the dos – that is, with the shooter – a number of players like to bet with the don'ts. This means placing an opening bet on the don't-pass line, in the same way that do betters place their bets on the pass line. If you place a **"wrong"** bet, as it is sometimes known, you win or lose in exact reverse to the **"right"** betters (see come-out roll and come-line bets, pages 38 and 42):

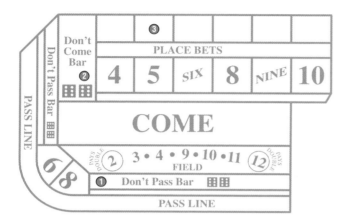

Don't betters place their initial bets on the don't-pass line (1) and don't-come bets in the don't-come box (2). Once the point has been established, the bet is moved to a space above the relevant place-bets box (3).

Example of a come-line betting scenario

- **If the shooter throws a 7 or an 11** on the come-out roll, you lose automatically.

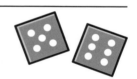

- **If the shooter throws a 2 or 3** on the come-out roll you win automatically, at odds of 1 to 1.

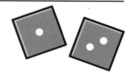

- **If the shooter throws a 12**, you tie. This means you keep your bet, but win nothing.

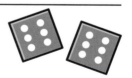

- **If the shooter throws a 4, 5, 6, 8, 9, or 10**, this is his point and you win if he throws a 7 before throwing that point again.

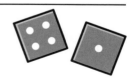

The real advantage to the don't better comes after the come-out roll, once the shooter has established his point, since the odds are now in favor of the throw resulting in a 7 before any other point. You can remove a don't-pass-line bet at any time. Just as you can take free odds on the pass line, you can lay odds on the don't-pass line (see below). To do this, instead of placing your odds bet behind the line bet, you place it on top and to one side instead.

Don't-come bets

These are made in exactly the same way as come-line bets, but in reverse: a new don't-come bet wins automatically if the shooter throws a 2 or 3, and draws on 12; the bet loses automatically if the shooter throws a 7 or 11. Should the shooter throw any point (4, 5, 6, 8, 9, 10), the bet is moved to a spot above the place-bet box for that number, awaiting a throw either of a 7 (to win) or that point (to lose). You can lay odds on these bets, but the payout is the same as for don't-pass-line bets (see below).

Gambler beware: Laying odds on the don'ts

While the pass-line better has favorable free odds when betting after the come-out roll, the odds are reversed for the don't-pass-line better, because he is backing the 7 to win. This means that you are always betting more chips than you stand to win:

• You have to bet 6 chips on a 6 or 8 to earn 5 chips (odds of 5 to 6 – because there are six chances of rolling a 7, as opposed to five chances of rolling a 6 or 8).

• You have to bet 9 chips on a 5 or 9 to earn 6 chips (odds of 2 to 3 – because there are six chances of rolling a 7, as opposed to four chances of rolling a 6 or 8).

• You have to bet 10 chips on a 4 or 10 to earn 5 chips (odds of 1 to 2 – because there are six chances of rolling a 7, as opposed to three chances of rolling a 4 or 10).

Place bets

Place bets can be made at any point in the game, although they are suspended on a come-out roll. This is a straight bet on any of the numbers 4, 5, 6, 8, 9, or 10 being rolled before a 7. You do not place the bet yourself, but ask a dealer to do it for you. If the shooter rolls that number before a 7, you win. The odds on these bets are paid at 9 to 5 for a roll of 4 or 10; at 7 to 5 for a roll of 5 or 9; and at 7 to 6 for a roll of 6 or 8 – and you should bet in multiples of 5, 5, and 6, respectively, to get maximum payout (see page 41). You should be aware that the house edge on these payouts varies tremendously: on a 4 or 10, the house edge is 6.7 percent; on a 9 or 5 it is 4 percent, and on the 6 or 8 it is 1.5 percent. This last is, therefore, the most advantageous place bet to make. Once you make a place bet, you do not have to leave it there until your number comes up – you can have it returned to you by the dealer at any time.

Field bets

Another bet that can be made at any point of the game is that in which a player can make a bet on the 2, 3, 4, 9, 10, 11, or 12 appearing before a 5, 6, 7, or 8, with a win paying even money on 3, 4, 9, 10, and 11 and 2 to 1 on 2 and 12. This appears to be a good bet, because it covers seven of eleven possible outcomes. However, this assumption overlooks the number of times each throw is possible. The 2, 3, 4, 9, 10, 11, or 12 will appear 16 times, while the remaining numbers can be made 20 different ways. This gives the house a clear advantage of 5.5 percent.

Big 6 and 8

We have seen already that these two numbers are the most frequent ones rolled after a 7, and that they can be a good bet. By making this bet – that the 6 or 8 will be rolled before a 7 – you earn an even-money payout on a win. The house edge is 9 percent. This bet is, however, effectively the same as a place bet on the 6 or 8, which is paid at odds of 7 to 6. With the place bet available to you, there is no reason to bet on big 6 or big 8 at all.

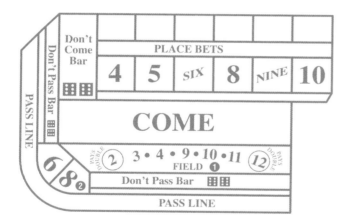

Field bets (1) and the Big 6/Big 8 (2) bets appear favorable at first glance, but prove less so on balance.

Winners and losers

In 1983, having recently lost $50,000 at Binion's Horseshoe, Las Vegas, high roller Robert Bergstrom returned to the craps table with $777,000 and bet the full amount on the pass line. The shooter made a point of 9, rolled a couple of other numbers, then another 9. Bergstrom had just doubled his money. A few weeks later he did the same again, betting and winning $548,000 on the pass line. Not long after that, Bergstrom placed a final bet at the craps table in Binion's Horseshoe, betting $1 million on the pass line. A huge crowd looked on as the shooter rolled a 9 to establish her point, followed by a 6/Ace. Bergstrom had lost the lot.

Buying a bet

It is possible to "buy" a bet instead of placing it (see page 45). This works in exactly the same way – that is, you let the dealer know which of the numbers 4, 5, 6, 8, 9, or 10 you want to bet on being rolled before a 7. He takes your chips and puts them in the appropriate box with a "buy" disc on top of the stake. The difference in buying a bet is that you get paid the true odds if you win (see page 41). The catch is that you pay a 5 percent commission to the casino. Whereas there is no house edge on free-odds bets, the commission when buying a bet gives the casino an edge of 4.76 percent. This means that buying a bet is only more favorable than placing a bet on the points 4 and 10.

Proposition bets

The collective proposition bets come under the jurisdiction of the stickman. During play, he will shout out the various bets that can be made, trying to persuade punters to place a bet on the shooter throwing a double six, or any crap, for example. Looking at the betting layout, it is easy to see that the payouts for these bets look lucrative: 15 to 1 on a throw of 3, for example, would win you 75 chips on a 5-chip bet. But it is worth taking a closer look at the odds. Since each of these bets is resolved on one roll, it is easy to work out the true odds in each case. A roll of double six or double one, for example has odds of 35 to 1 – not the 30 to 1 payout. This gives the house an advantage of as much as 13.9 percent. A hardway bet is on a point being made with a double – for example, hardway 8 is a double 4. All throws have similar, shortened odds, giving the house a substantial advantage every time (ranging from 9.1 percent (hard 8/hard 6) to 16.7 percent (any seven).

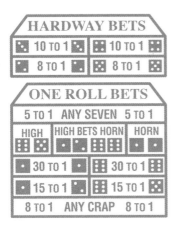

The proposition bets offer the worst payouts on the betting layout, leaving the casino with a considerable house edge.

Poker

Poker

Poker is currently more popular than it has ever been before. Until the end of the 20th century the game was considered a particularly American pastime, but now, thanks largely to the Internet and the broadcasting of global poker tournaments, is catching on fast worldwide. The origin of the name poker is thought to derive from the game "poque," which was being played around New Orleans *c.*1800, while under French rule.

The game as we know it today was first played in America, *c.*1850, and is thought to have its origins in a number of earlier European games, the most notable of which being "bouillotte," a 19th-century game from France. Other games associated with early forms of poker are a Persian game called "as-nas" and the French game "poque," both of which were played along similar lines to bouillotte. All of these games had similar principles at their core – most obviously the dealing of five cards, the ranking of those cards, and the betting set-ups that were used.

First played in the US with a 20-card pack (A, K, Q, J, 10 in each suit) and four players, it was not long before one version of the game was being played with the full pack of 52 cards. By 1850, this form had completely overtaken the 20-card game and was briefly known as "bluff."

As with all types of gambling, poker was associated with the **cardsharps and gangsters** of the Mississippi river casinos, although towards the end of the 19th century it was more widely played as a respectable and entertaining private game in homes among friends and acquaintances. The 20th century saw the emergence of casinos and clubs as important places to play, and some high-stake casino games played by experts receive wide publicity and are closely followed by the press.

The casino setup

Unlike any other casino game, poker is played by a number of players who bet against each other – not the house – to win the money staked as chips during the game. The casino provides a room, away from the main action of the casino, and a dealer for the game. For games in which the position of the dealer moves with each hand, a button is used to designate one of the players each time. Because there is no way of profiting from a house edge, casinos take their revenue from poker in a number of ways: they often charge players rent for the room and staff provided; they may also charge seat rental – an hourly fee per player (sometimes increasing with the betting limits); and they often take a commission from the "pot" for each deal (usually 10 to 15 percent.)

Poker basics

There are many variations of poker, including **seven-card stud** and **Texas hold'em**, each of which involves more cards being taken during play, but the resulting poker hand always contains just five cards. Although rules of play differ slightly, depending on which version of the game is being played, all games share a number of common practices.

The object of the game

Winning money, or the chips representing money, from the other players is the object of the game. This is achieved in a succession of deals in which players bet or fold depending on their cards. Each deal is complete in itself and is not affected by previous or subsequent deals. Play continues until an agreed time or until only one player remains in the game – all others having lost their stake money.

The number of players

Depending on which version of poker is being played, the number of players can vary from two to fourteen. Players may join a game that has already started, so it is usual at the start of the game to agree a maximum number. When the maximum number of people is playing, no one else can join until one of the current players leaves. Players can decide at the beginning of a game not to admit latecomers.

The deal

A standard pack of 52 cards is used, where each suit is equal and the cards rank according to their face or pip value, with Aces being either high or low: (A), K, Q, J, 10, 9, 8, 7, 6, 5, 4, 3, 2 (A). Some versions allow the use of wild cards, but these are primarily restricted to domestic games (see page 136).

A casino dealer shuffles the cards and deals each player (starting to his left) with a minimum of five cards: in some games, more cards are dealt from which the players select a five-card poker hand. In successive rounds of betting, each player bets that he holds a better poker hand than any other player. Players place their bets in front of them, towards the center of the table, the accumulated bets becoming the **"pot."** A player may fold (pull out of a deal) at any time, thereby losing any stakes he has already bet in that deal.

A deal finishes when either all players but one fold, and he takes the pot, or a showdown is reached: the remaining players reveal their hands and the player with the best hand takes the pot.

Poker-hand ranks

The ranking of poker hands is universal and applies to all versions of the game. From the highest to the lowest, they are as follows:

Royal flush

Rank 1 The five highest-ranking cards of the same suit. A tie is possible.

Straight flush

Rank 2 Five cards of the same suit in sequence. Between two or more straight flushes, that with the highest-ranking top card wins. A tie is possible.

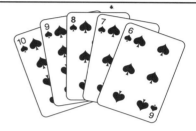

Four of a kind

Rank 3 Four cards of the same rank, with an odd fifth card. Between two similar hands, that with the higher-ranking four cards wins. There cannot be a tie, so the fifth card is of no consequence.

Full house

Rank 4 Three cards of one rank (a triple) and two of another (a pair). Between two full houses, the one with the higher-ranking set of three wins. A tie is impossible.

Flush

Rank 5 Five cards of the same suit, but not in sequence. Between flushes, the one containing the highest card wins. If equal, the second highest and so on. Ties are possible.

Straight

Rank 6 Five cards in a sequence, but not of the same suit. Between straights, the one containing the highest card at the top of the sequence wins. Note that A, K, Q, J, 10 beats 5, 4, 3, 2, A, where the Ace counts as low. Ties are possible.

Three of a kind

Rank 7 Three cards of the same rank with two non-matching cards. Between similar hands, the one with the highest-ranking triple wins. Ties are impossible.

Two pairs

Rank 8 Two cards of one rank, two of another, and one odd card. Between similar hands, that with the highest-ranking pair wins. If equal, the highest-ranking second pair. If the second pair is equal, the highest-ranking odd card wins the hand. Ties are possible.

One pair

Rank 9 Two cards of one rank with three other non-matching cards. Between similar hands, the highest-ranking pair wins. If equal, the highest-ranking odd card and so on. Ties are possible.

Nothing

Rank 10 This hand lacks an accepted name, and is sometimes called a no-pair hand or a high-card hand. Hands of this type are ranked by the highest card they contain, if equal, the second highest, and so on. Ties are possible.

Betting options

In all forms of poker, betting takes place in **"betting intervals"** at specific points in the game. Each time, one player has the right or obligation to start the betting, which he will do by placing a number of chips in the pot at the center of the table, stating that number as he does so: for example, "I bet one." After this, play continues to the left. When it comes to his turn, any player has one of the following betting options.

Call

The player puts enough chips into the pot to make his stake so far equal to that of the highest better. He announces his move, and the number of chips he puts in: "I call for two." This keeps him in the game.

Raise

The player puts enough chips into the pot to make his stake equal to the highest better, but then adds an extra number of chips. He announces his move, and the number of chips he puts in: "I call two and raise another two." This raises the stakes and subsequent players must call to stay in the game. The betting interval is over only once all players left in the game have put in equal stakes.

Fold

The player feels unable to compete in this hand and returns his cards, face down, to the dealer. He announces he is folding and takes no further participation in that deal. He loses any money he has already staked and his interest in winning the pot.

Checking

In some forms of poker, players have an option to **"check."** In any given betting interval, the first player to bet can check – that is he can stay in the game without making a bet. Subsequent players can also check, but only for as long as nobody bets. Once a player makes a bet, all other players must call, raise, or fold until all bets in that interval are equal.

Profile of a poker player

The seasoned poker player is more than likely a professional gambler and displays considerable skill at the table. He has a good many years' experience behind him and has no trouble scanning the table to see which cards have been dealt and what his chances of winning are from what remains. Psyching out other players is a hobby, and spotting "tells" – some action or aspect of a player's body language that reveals information about his hand – has become second nature. He himself gives nothing away and there is nothing to rival bluffing on a great hand and finding a strategy to keep those opponents betting.

Antes and blinds

An ante is the number of chips put into the middle of the table before each deal – usually 1 chip per player – in order to make the game more rewarding financially. However, the practice is not commonly employed in casino games, and is more likely to be used in domestic poker (see page 135).

In other poker games, such as Texas hold'em (see pages 68–79), a blind bet is made by each of the first two players to the dealer's left. The first player puts in a **small blind** (say, 1 chip) and the second puts in a **big blind** (say, 2 chips). The third player starts the regular betting procedure, and he must put in at least 2 chips to start (effectively calling the big blind). When the first round of betting is complete, the small and big blinds will be counted as part of the first bets of players 1 and 2 respectively. For example, if the stake is now at 6 chips, player 1 must add a further 5 chips to call, and player 2 must add 4 chips.

Poker terminology

Ante A compulsory bet placed into the pot before the deal.

Betting interval The periods in a game where players must bet, raise, call, check, or fold.

Betting limit The minimum or maximum number of chips a player is allowed to bet.

Betting round Each betting interval comprises a number of betting rounds, in which each player has the opportunity to bet once. Once all have done so, the player who bet first has the option of betting again and a second betting round begins. Successive rounds take place until all bets are equal, when the betting interval ends.

Blind A compulsory bet made before the deal. It is an active bet – that is, it counts towards the better's total stake.

Chips Tokens used in poker instead of money.

Loose player A player who bets in defiance of the odds.

Pot The total of the stakes that have been bet, and the amount that the winner takes.

Showdown The display of cards at the end of a hand to determine the winner.

Side pot A separate pot begun when a player taps out.

Tap out The situation when a player is forced to suspend his betting because he has insufficient chips to call the bet.

Tell A subconscious signal that lets other players know the strength of your hand.

Tight player A player who bets only on strong hands.

Wild card A card which, by prior agreement, its holder can use as any card he wishes.

Betting interval

A betting interval can last a number of rounds, depending on how the betting goes. The interval will not be over until all players left in the game have bet the same number of chips. Consider the following scenario, for example.

Round 1

- Player 1 bets 1 chip.
- Player 2 folds.
- Player 3 calls and raises one, putting in 2 chips.
- Player 4 calls, putting in 2 chips.
- Player 5 calls, putting in 2 chips.
- Player 6 call and raises, putting in 4 chips.

After the first betting round, player 2 is already out of the game. Another round of betting starts, again, with player 1.

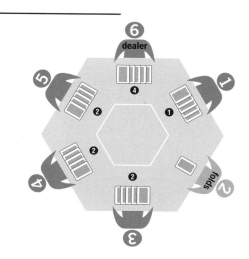

Round 2

- Player 1 calls. The betting is up to 4 chips, and player 1 has a stake of 1 chip so far, so he must now add 3 chips to stay in the game.
- Player 3 calls and raises 2, adding 4 chips to his stake in total.
- Player 4 folds.
- Player 5 calls, adding 4 chips to his stake.
- Player 6 folds.

Two more players are now out of the game. The third round of betting starts.

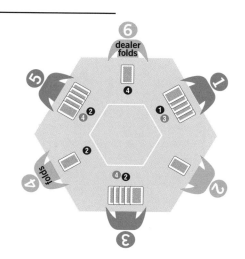

Round 3

- Player 1 folds.
- Player 3 checks.
- Player 5 checks.

The players left in the game have bet the same number of chips and their stakes are equal. There are 22 chips in the pot and it is now time for the showdown (see page 61).

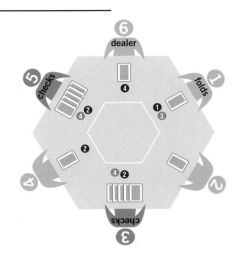

Betting limits

In a casino, each poker table will have a betting minimum and maximum, and you should choose a table to suit your pocket. Be quite sure you have understood the table rules for betting and raising, as they vary and the implications can be crippling. The following sections outline popular betting setups and show how they can escalate once play is in swing.

● 1st-round stakes
● 2nd-round stakes

1-chip limit

All bets and raises may be limited to a given number of chips. Even if the limit was 1 chip, it is possible for stakes to rise swiftly if a number of players are betting. The pot at the end of this betting interval has a total of 51 chips.

	Player 1	Player 2	Player 3	Player 4	Player 5
Round 1	Bets 1 chip	Raises 1 to 2	Raises 1 to 3	Raises 1 to 4	Raises 1 to 5
Round 2	Raises 1 to 6 (adding 5 chips)	Raises 1 to 7 (adding 5 chips)	Raises 1 to 8 (adding 5 chips)	Raises 1 to 9 (adding 5 chips)	Raises 1 to 10 (adding 5 chips)
Round 3	Raises 1 to 11 (adding 5 chips)	Calls 11 (adding 4 chips)	Folds	Calls 11 (adding 2 chips)	Folds

Betting the raise

With this setup, each player has the option to raise by the maximum number of chips staked by a player so far. For example, if player 1 bets 1 chip, the limit for a raise is 1 chip. The first player to raise must put in 2 chips (1 to call and 1 to raise) – the limit is now 2 chips (the highest stake so far) with the limit rising as the betting progresses. Players do not have to bet up to the limit, but were they to do so, stakes would rise rapidly (see table, where each player either folds, calls, or raises by the maximum).

	Player 1	**Player 2**	**Player 3**	**Player 4**	**Player 5**
Round 1	Bets 1 chip raises 1	Calls (1) and raises 2 (2)	Calls (2) and raises 4 (4)	Calls (4) and raises 4 (8)	Calls (8) and raises 8 (16)
Round 2	Calls (15) and raises 16 Limit now 31	Folds	Calls (27) and raises 31 Limit now 58	Folds	Calls (38) and raises 58 Limit now 96
Round 3	Folds		Calls (38)		

Betting increases

In some games, the betting limit is raised with each new betting interval in any one deal. For example, the initial bet may be 1 chip, with a raise in the first betting interval at 2 chips; in the second betting interval at 5 chips; and in the third betting interval at 10 chips.

Table stakes

Each player buys an agreed equal amount of chips from the casino before play starts. This is called the **"take-out."** If a player wants more chips, he has to buy them in the same amount of chips each time – say 100. He cannot buy additional chips in the middle of a deal, and if he runs out he must wait until that deal has been won. He can only buy fewer than the original amount of chips if he cannot afford to buy more. If he then loses these chips he must leave the game. A player who runs out of chips during a deal must "tap out" (see page 59).

In some casinos, to begin with all players have the same number of chips and play until there is only one player left – who wins the lot. In this situation, nobody can buy more chips during the game.

Tapping out

Tapping out is a practice in poker that safeguards against smaller players being pushed out of a game by high rollers. If a player runs out of chips during a deal – say, he has 6 chips and needs 8 to call – he can call for 6, adding his chips to the pot, and tap out. Any excess already paid by the other players is moved to a side pot, where the betting continues until the end of the deal. The player who tapped out continues to play, competing for the main pot, but does not place any more bets. At the showdown, all remaining players – including the one who tapped out – compete for the main pot, while the **side pot** is contested only by the players who continued the betting. However, a player who folds in the side pot cannot compete for the main pot. The following shows an example of a betting interval in which one player taps out.

Round 1

- Player 1 checks.
- Betting starts with player 2 and is up to 4 chips by the end of the round.
- The dealer folds.

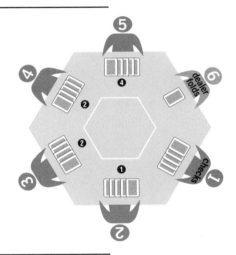

Round 2

- Play continues with player 1, who calls.
- Players 2, 3, and 5 continue to bet, while player 4 folds.
- The stakes are now at 12 chips.

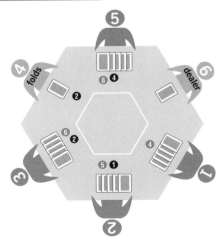

- ● 1st-round stakes
- ● 2nd-round stakes
- ● 3rd-round stakes
- ● 4th-round stakes
- ○ side pot

Round 3

- Player 1 has only 6 chips remaining but wants to stay in the game. He taps out with a total of 10 chips, two fewer than he needs to call.
- Players 2 and 3 add sufficient chips to bring their main-pot stakes up to 10, and put 2 chips in a side pot.
- Player 5 takes 2 chips from his main-pot stake (to make his bet equal to all others) and moves them to a side pot.

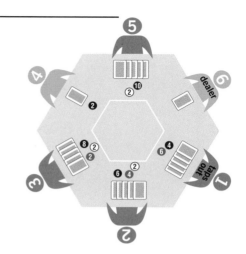

Round 4

- From this point on, all stakes contribute to the side pot. Player 1 is still in the game, but no longer betting, so play continues with player 2. He raises 2 chips. Player 3 folds and player 5 calls, adding 2 chips to the side pot.

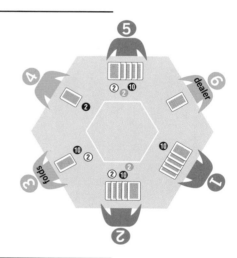

The showdown

- There are three players left in the game – 1, 2, and 5. The showdown reveals that player 1 has the strongest hand with a full house, so he wins the main pot (42 chips). Player 2's flush is the next strongest hand and he takes the side pot (10 chips).

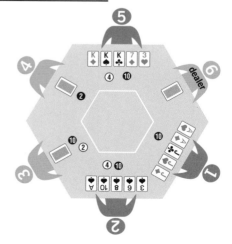

- ● main pot
- ● 2nd-round stakes
- ● 3rd-round stakes
- ● 4th-round stakes
- ○ side pot

The showdown

When all betting intervals are over, the players still in the game reveal their cards, starting with the last player to raise. He will announce his hand, for example "royal flush," as he does so. The player with the highest-ranking poker hand (see pages 52–53) wins the pot. Should any of the players make a false announcement in error – say, by calling "three of a kind" when he in fact has a full house – he is not bound by his announcement: play is determined by the cards alone.

If two or more players tie, they share the pot. An odd chip that cannot be divided goes to the last person to raise the stakes. If there is only one player remaining by the end of the last betting interval, there is no need for a showdown. The player takes the pot and is not obliged to show his hand.

If only one player remains in the game – that is, he bet and no other player subsequently called – there is no need to have a showdown at all. That player simply takes the pot without even having to reveal his cards. In all scenarios, a player should not take the pot before it is agreed by the other players that he has won it.

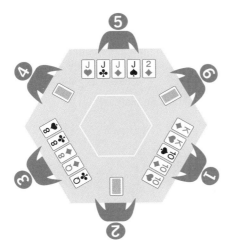

In this example, players 1 and 3 had strong hands, each with a full house. Player 5, however, has four of a kind and wins the pot.

General poker strategy

A good deal of poker is about math. The probability of being dealt certain hands and the likelihood of improving a hand in a certain way always comes down to the number of cards in the pack, which ones have already been dealt, and the number still remaining. No matter what hand you have and what hand you think your opponents have, there are times when betting will depend on:

1 The chances of your hand being a winning one, and
2 The amount of money it stands to win.

For example, a 3 to 1 chance that will win you six times your stake is a good bet, while a 6 to 1 chance that you will win three times your stake is a bad one. In some forms of poker it is possible to work out from the cards already seen which cards are left in the pack, and what your chances are of getting a favorable hand (see Omaha, page 84, for a working example of this).

Although there is most definitely an element of luck in the game of poker, a good many wins are largely down to the skill of the individual. In addition to a general familiarity with the numerical aspects of poker – the various combinations possible and the likelihood of achieving them – players must also consider the psychological aspects of playing poker if they want to win consistently. A good player needs to be able to study the behavior of the other players at the table, and to play his game accordingly:

• Are the other players at the table good players or bad players?

• Are the other players tight or loose players (see opposite)?

• Does any one of them betray his cards by showing excitement or by repeating behavior he had with a previous good hand?

• Do you have a pattern of behavior that gives too much away?

• Can you tell when another player is bluffing?

Gambler beware

Never be tempted to throw good money after bad. There will be times when you have a good hand and have bet accordingly, only to learn too late in the game that your hand is unlikely to win. There is nothing to be gained from trying to protect the money you have put in the pot so far by risking more. It is an important lesson to learn that the money you stake is no longer yours once it reaches the center of the table.

Winners and losers

In 2003, amateur poker player Chris Moneymaker shook the gaming world when he won the World Series of Poker (WSOP) (see page 73), having never played in a real tournament before. Before competing, he had played the game exclusively on the Internet – in fact, it was through winning a $39-buy-in tournament on the Internet that Moneymaker came to be playing in the WSOP at all. His final game was played against one Ihsan "Sam" Farha from Texas. The hole cards – those that are dealt face down – were dealt, giving Moneymaker a 4/5 and Farha 10/J. The flop followed: J/4/5. Moneymaker now had two pairs to Farha's pair of Jacks. Farha bet everything he had – more than $1 million and Moneymaker called. The men watched as the dealer dealt the turn (8) and the river (5). Incredibly, Moneymaker had a full house and took the $2.5 million prize.

Tight and loose players

A **"tight"** player is one who will bet only when he has a good hand, and is prepared to wait for one to come along. If a player is known to be a tight player, whenever he suddenly starts to bet on a hand, an aware opponent will know he holds something worthwhile and is likely to fold where he might have raised a chip or two on a moderate hand. When among good players, a tight player will earn fewer chips when he gets a good hand than he might have done if he had, once in a while, shown more inclination to take a risk.

A **"loose"** player is one who will sometimes get impatient to be in the action and will bet somewhat impetuously. A loose player, known to bet on straights or flushes of three cards in the hope that he will fill later in the game, will not scare anyone into folding.

A good player will be aware of the temperaments of his opponents and will act accordingly, at the same time trying to ensure that he plays a varied game himself.

Bluffing in poker

Bluffing is considered one of the most important elements of playing poker, no matter which version you are playing. When it comes to the showdown, there is no doubt that the best hand always wins the pot, but there is no guarantee that this is the best hand that was held by any player during the deal. In many cases, the holder of the best hand is bluffed into folding before the showdown.

Bluffing in poker involves **misleading the other players** in the game regarding the value of your hand, and there are two common ways of achieving this:

1 You bet heavily to persuade the other players that your hand is, in fact, better than it actually is. If you bet heavily enough, opponents will fold rather than risk losing more chips to call, and you can win the pot – sometimes with the poorest hand at the table. Your aim with this kind of bluff is to avoid a showdown, and it is most successful when the table limits are high, and players have to risk a large number of chips to call the bluff. With lower limits, an opponent is more likely to be tempted to call you and your bluff will almost certainly fail.

2 You persuade the other players that your hand is less good than it actually is. This way, more players stay in the game for longer and contribute more chips to the pot. Come the showdown, you have the chance of winning a significant jackpot.

Double bluff

In most instances, if you avoid a showdown – as in the first example – you do not have to expose your hand to the other players and opponents will not know that you have called a bluff. However, on some occasions, you can make it work to your advantage if a successful bluff is revealed. For example, you could successfully avoid a showdown in one deal, but reveal your poor hand to the frustration of the other players. When you get a good hand, you can employ method 2 above – betting hard and raising the stakes. Remembering the last bluff, an opponent with a reasonable hand

Gambler beware

It is generally accepted that it is harder to bluff a poor player than it is a good one. If you hold a poor hand and are behaving as if you have a strong one, a good player is likely to spot your behavior and possibly fold. The very same bluff might go over the head of a poor player, who will be more inclined to call, to your horror. There is no point in trying to bluff poor players, thus courting disaster, when you can probably beat them legitimately anyway.

Bluffing tips

Bluffing is harder than it might sound and it can be expensive when you do not pull it off. For more likely success, consider the following:

Number of players The more players left in the game, the harder it is to pull off a successful bluff. One-on-one can be more intimidating, but it is difficult to force three or more players out of a potential showdown.

Position Being the last to speak in a round is the best position for pulling off a bluff. You can see how all the other players have bet, and if there is a weakness – say only one player has bet – a raise from you may well put others off.

Your opponents It pays to take a little time to see what kind of players you are up against. A bad player might be scared of losing to a bluff, and might call whatever the circumstances. Similarly, newcomers to the game are particularly irritated by players who bluff and will often call to spoil your chances of success.

Table limits Some games are better suited to a good bluff than others – in general, those in which the limits are highest, or where there is no limit at all. For example, few players are prepared to be bluffed out of a 100-chip pot if all it costs to stay in is 5 chips. And the bigger the pot grows in a low-limit game, the harder it will be to pull off a bluff.

may be tempted to stay with you and force a showdown, which, on this occasion, you win, with a bigger pot than you might otherwise have hoped for.

Bluffing to look weak

This technique is best played in limit poker, where you need to build up the pot you intend to win. You therefore bet slowly, sometimes calling when you might have raised, to encourage other players to stay in the game longer. You must be sure of your hand and that it is, in fact, likely to be the best in the game. There are two potential pitfalls:

1 If you bet the maximum at every opportunity you run the risk of the other players folding, which would leave you with a lower pot than you would like.
2 If you bet too low, and nobody raises, you run the risk of not making the most of your hand.

Poker etiquette

Large sums of money can change hands very quickly in poker and this can make for a game of high emotions and possibly strong disputes. In order to standardize the game, and avoid unnecessary arguments, a number of points should be observed regarding etiquette:

- Play should be seen to be above board at all times.

- It is not acceptable to criticize the dealer.

- Each player is responsible for his own cards, and should have them in view at all times. He should not touch another player's cards or another player's chips.

- No player should keep a stash of chips in his pockets – they should be on the table at all times.

- Cards that are not intended for viewing should remain so. If a player folds, he should make sure his cards are always returned to the dealer face down.

- In most forms of poker a player should only reveal his cards during the showdown.

- It is rare at a casino for losers to show their hands, and experienced players will not ask them to do so even though they are entitled to see all of the cards following a showdown.

- A player should not discuss his hand at any point during the game, even if he has folded, neither should players discuss a hand once it is over.

Betting out of turn

Betting out of turn in poker can influence play and is not welcome. Should it happen, the offending player's call is **"frozen"** for the time being and play continues as if the call has not been made. When his proper turn to bet comes around, he has a number of options:
- If he bet, and there was no previous bet in that interval, his bet counts.
- If there has been an intervening bet, he is deemed to have called. If the chips he put in were insufficient for the call, he must add to them. If he does not wish to add to

them, he must fold, forfeiting his out-of-turn bet to the pot. He cannot retrieve chips if his bet was in excess of that required to call, and he cannot raise.
- If a player folds out of turn, he must put in the required chips to call any raise made by a player who had yet to act when he folded. He is still deemed to have folded and has no stake in the pot.

Betting on a certainty

Some poker schools think it is bad etiquette for a player who is holding an unbeatable hand (for example, the hole cards that complete the best-possible hand when combined with the board in Texas hold'em or Omaha) to continue to bet. Some might argue that it is unfair to take money from fellow players by betting on a certainty. On the other hand, if you cannot exploit the best hands to accrue the most money, what is poker about? Nobody is forced to bet against you.

- It is considered bad behavior to take too long over a decision in a betting interval – some casinos may impose a time limit.

- A player must always state clearly whether he is betting, folding, calling, or raising, and the number of chips he is putting in the pot.

- When placing chips in the pot, you should not mix your chips with those of anyone else, and you should put all the chips you intend to bet in at once, without going back to your stash for more – it must always be clear how many chips you have put in already, and how many you are adding at any one time.

- If a player makes a bet or call, but puts no chips into the pot, his move is void.

- If a player makes a bet or call, but puts insufficient chips into the pot, he must on demand add the necessary chips.

- A player who puts in too many chips in error, can rectify the mistake only before another player points out the error. If someone else spots the error first, the chips are forfeited.

- Players should not discard cards, or make an action indicating their intent to do so, out of turn.

- A player should treat all other players at the table alike. He should not bet more gently against a friend than he would against another.

Texas hold'em

This is the best-known version of poker played in casinos, largely because it is the form played in the televised global tournaments in both the US and the UK. The object of the game is for each player to make the best poker hand from two cards dealt to him face down (**"hole cards"**) and five **"community"** cards dealt face up in the center of the table during play. Any combination is possible in achieving this – that is, players are not obliged to use their hole cards.

The role of the dealer is significant for the order of betting in this game, so although the casino provides a dealer to distribute the cards the table also has a **"notional"** dealer, indicated by a disc or button that passes counterclockwise around the table to each player in turn with each deal. The casino dealer always shuffles the cards and burns the top card before play.

Before any cards are dealt, the two players to the left of the notional dealer each stake a blind bet (see page 55). The first player makes a **"small blind:"** a percentage of the minimum bet – usually a half or a third. The second player makes a **"big blind:"** the minimum bet.

Order of play

Following the posting, or pushing to the center of the table, of the blind bets, the casino dealer deals each player two cards face down, and betting begins.

First betting interval

Each player examines his cards and betting starts with the player to the left of the big blind. He must call, raise, or fold, but is not allowed to check (see page 54) because the blind bets have been made. As the betting goes around the table, players 1 and 2 must also call, raise, or fold. Both will have to raise their stakes to the current level of betting in order to call, and add more to raise. With more than one player raising on his turn, the betting may go around the table several times before all the bets of those players remaining in are equal, at which point the betting interval ends.

The flop

When all bets are equal, the dealer burns the top card of the pack and deals three community cards, face up, in the center of the table. These three cards are known as the **"flop."** A second betting interval now takes place, and starts with the nearest active player – one who has not folded – to the notional dealer's left.

The turn
When all bets are again equal, the casino dealer once more burns the top card and deals another community card, face up, in the center of the table. This is called the **"turn"** or **"fourth street."**

The river
Following another betting interval, a final top card is burned and the last community card is dealt, face up, to the center of the table. This is called the **"river"** or **"fifth street."** The final betting interval takes place, and then the showdown.

Hold'em terminology

Back door A player who, usually inadvertently, completes a flush or a straight with the last two community cards is said to have done so "by the back door."

Big blind The player to the small blind's left, who before the deal also makes a blind bet of an agreed amount – usually two or three times that of the small blind. It also refers to the bet itself.

Board The term used to describe the complete set of five community cards, placed face up at the center of the table.

Community cards Any of the five cards dealt face up in the center of the table by the casino dealer. These cards can be used by any of the players in making the best poker hand.

Flop The first three of the community cards, dealt face up.

Hole cards The two cards dealt face down to each player at the beginning of the game.

Kicker The lower of the two hole cards each player holds.

Notional dealer The player who would be dealer for any given round in the absence of the casino dealer, indicated by a disc or button that rotates around the table.

Nuts (nut hand) The best possible hand in the game, taking into account the player's hole cards and the five community cards.

On the button The notional dealer for any deal is said to be "on the button."

River (fifth street) The fifth community card.

Small blind The player to the dealer's left, who, before the deal, makes a blind bet of an agreed amount. It also refers to the bet itself.

Suited If a player's two hole cards are of the same suit, they are said to be suited.

Turn (fourth street) The fourth community card.

The "nuts"

Once all community cards have been dealt (the whole set of five is known collectively as the board) each player should consider which two cards could be added to it to make the best hand possible, referred to as the **"nuts."** For example with the following board – Q ♣, J ♣, J ♠, 10 ♣, 9 ♦ – the best hole cards would be A ♣ and K ♣ for a royal flush. If these are lacking, each player should consider the next best hand. In this case a full house, a flush, and a straight are all quite likely possibilities.

Nut hand

The deal

In each case, a player must use three community cards and his two hole cards to make the best hand. In this example, the nuts or nut hand would be an Ace-high straight.

The flop

The turn

The river

The nuts

Example of a basic hand

The following example shows each step of a given hand with five players. Player 1 is the notional dealer, player 2 is the small blind and player 3 the big blind.

Stake limits

Small blind: 1 chip.
Big blind: 3 chips.
Minimum bet or raise: 3 chips.
Maximum first-round bet or raise: 10 chips.
Maximum subsequent-round bet or raise: 20 chips.

First betting interval

- Player 1 is on the button, player 2 is small blind, and player 3 is big blind.
- Player 4 is the first player to call, raise, or fold. He has a poor hand and folds.
- Player 5 has a reasonably good hand – 10, 9 suited (of the same suit) – and calls.
- Player 1 calls with a small pair.
- Player 2 has a very good hand – A, Q suited. He made a small blind of 1 chip, so adds 2 to call and 3 to raise.
- The remaining players, including player 3 who already had 3 chips in as big blind, call. There are 24 chips in the pot and four players still in the game.

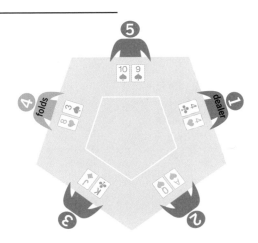

Player 2 has a good enough hand to bet positively straight away.

Tip

Remember that the community cards are not just at your disposal, but are available to every player at the table. If a pair of Aces appears in the flop – everyone will benefit from that. Your hole cards need to be strong enough to compete as play continues. For example if you have J♥/10♥ and the flop is A♣/A♦/4♣, you are unlikely to be holding the best hand.

Second betting interval

- The flop is made: J♠; Q♣; J♣.
- Player 2 has lost his chance of a flush with the flop, but now has two pairs (Q, J). He bets 3 to check.
- Player 3 has the best hand at the table so far: 3 Jacks, but also a J, Q, K♣. Not wanting to draw attention to a good hand at this stage, he calls.
- Player 5 calls with a double-ended straight (Q, J, 10, 9) and three spades.
- Player 1 has a poor hand with two pairs. The other players also have the pair of Jacks and his pair of 4s is low. He knows other players probably have stronger hands, but calls to stay in the game.
- With all bets equal, there are now 36 chips in the pot, and four players still in the game.

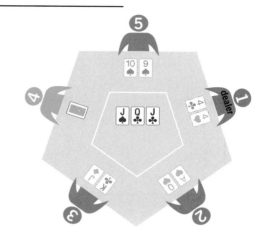

The flop has been particularly favorable to players 3 and 5.

Third betting interval

- With the turn, another card is added to the community cards in the center of the table – the 10♣.
- Player 2's hand does not improve and he checks.
- Player 3 now has K, Q, J, 10 suited and the possibility of a royal flush. He still has no better than three Jacks, but decides to put the pressure on by betting 20 chips.
- Player 5 now has two pairs – Jacks and 10s – and a potential Queen-high straight. He calls with 20 chips.
- Player 1 still has two pairs. Another club would give him a flush, but it could give any one of the other players a flush, too. His 4♣ would decide the outcome and is low. He folds.
- Player 2, who checked at the beginning of the betting, calls with 20 chips.
- With all bets equal, there are three players left in the game and 96 chips in the pot.

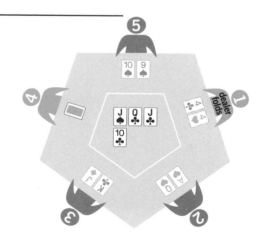

The turn is only of any real advantage to player 3.

Fourth betting interval

- The river reveals a 9♦ and completes the board of community cards.
- Player 2's best hand is still two pairs, and he checks.
- Player 3 has a straight, but cannot be certain it is enough to win the game – he checks, too.
- Player 5 has little confidence in his two pairs and checks as well, leaving three players in the showdown.
- Player 3 wins with his straight and takes the pot of 96 chips. Having bet 29 chips of his own, his profit is 67 chips.

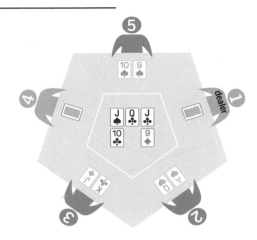

The straight beats both sets of two pairs and so player 3 takes the pot.

The World Series of Poker

In 1973, Benny Binion, the man behind the World Series of Poker (WSOP), mused over whether the number of competitors would reach as many as 50 in years to come. Since debuting in 1970, the tournament – staged to find the "World Champion" of the game – had attracted considerable attention and players had risen from seven in 1971 to 13 a year later, so 50 did not seem an unrealistic goal. Thanks to the phenomenal explosion in poker playing in the last decade, participants in the WSOP have way exceeded Binion's dreams. The 50-entrant tournament was realized in 1982. Just five years later there were 2,141 players. By 2005 no fewer than 5,600 took part, and each paid $10,000 for the privilege. The top 560 players won prize money on a sliding scale that guaranteed the nine finalists at least $1 million each. The winner of the 14-hour final was 39-year-old "unknown" Joseph Hachem, who had moved from Lebanon to Australia as a child. He gave up a career as a chiropractor to concentrate on poker in 2002. He won the biggest prize ever in poker – a cool $7.5 million. The second, another "unknown," took $4.25 million.

Strategy

In Texas hold'em, strategy starts with the hole cards. Every player at the table can use the five community cards, so it is down to each player's hole cards to make the best possible hand, potentially winning the game outright.

Hole cards

There is a limited number of combinations that can be made with the hole cards and they are considered essential in determining how a player should proceed in the first and subsequent betting intervals. The possible combinations were first ranked in the book *Hold'Em Poker* by David Sklansky in 1976, and have been used as a guide for poker players ever since.

Ranks for hole cards

Pair

A pair is a good start, as there is a chance of improving to three of a kind. When it comes to evaluating pairs, there are big gaps between each of the high pairs (Aces, Kings, and Queens). After this, Jacks, 10s, and 9s are considered medium pairs; and 8s and below small pairs.

Ace with high kicker

This is more valuable than a medium or small pair, particularly if suited. For example, if you have Ace/King and an Ace or King appear in the flop, you hold the top pair with the highest kicker. Ace/Queen will be beaten if an Ace flops and an opponent holds Ace/King. Ace with a medium kicker of Jack, 10, or 9 is also a good hand to bet on.

Ace with small kicker

Ace with a small kicker suited has potential for an Ace-high flush, so is valuable. With Ace/5 suited and three more suited cards in the board, you hold the top flush. An Ace with a small kicker that is not suited is not a good hand, ranking below a combination with potential flushes or straights.

Unpaired high cards

Suited unpaired high cards are better to
bet on than a small pair, as they have
flush and straight potential. Hands such
as King/Queen or King/Jack might look
favorable before the flop, but can lead
to problems, particularly if unsuited. For
example, King/Jack with a King in the flop
gives you a high-ranking pair. But a Jack
in the flop leaves you with a pair that is
easily beaten.

Suited and/or consecutive cards

Two suited or consecutive cards are called
"drawing hands" because you have a long
way to go to make a five-card straight or
flush. Consecutive and suited is better than
one or the other, with 9/8 down to 5/4
considered the same as a small pair. Suited
cards that cannot form a straight should be
folded. Consecutive, non-suited cards lower
than Queen/Jack are considered of less
value than a pair.

Other combinations

If neither of your two cards is high (Jack
and below), and if they are not suited and
there are gaps between them (Jack/4;
9/6), they should not be bet on. This does
not mean that all other hands are good –
for example, 7/6 unsuited or 3/2 suited are
equally poor hands.

Position in relation to the dealer

The notional dealer passes to the left with each
deal and this has a bearing on your strategy.
The dealer is the last to speak on all rounds
except the first, when big blind is the last to
speak. The closer you are to the dealer's right,
the better, because there are fewer players
to speak after you. This may well influence
how you bet. With a late betting position, you
can get a feeling for the strength of other

players' hands by the way they bet in the first
betting interval. After the flop, knowing how
the other players continue to bet will indicate
whether you can risk playing with a relatively
poor hand, where otherwise you might fold.
In general, to play with confidence, you need
a better hand when you have an early
betting position.

Before the flop

Players tend to have their own strategies when it comes to betting before the flop. You can see which are the best combinations of hole cards on pages 74–75. A tight player might only bet on a pair, or two cards higher than a 10, or a suited Ace. A looser player might also bet on two smaller cards if they are both suited and consecutive.

A poor flop

The flop is the point at which your game can be made or broken. A pair of good cards can be rendered useless by the flop, while a moderate hand can become very strong. Hoping to make straights or flushes, or continuing to play with a pair when there is a higher card in the flop is generally a bad bet, especially if there is no table or pot limit. You run the risk of competing against high rollers with a relatively poor hand and the stakes can increase very quickly.

Nothing from the flop

If you had a good hand before the flop, but it brings you nothing, then you should fold. In this example, your good opening hand Ace/10 suited has come to nothing. At best you have a pair of 8s. You should assume that another player will have at least a King or an 8, making two pairs or three of a kind, respectively. He, or another player, might even have King/8 as hole cards, in which case you are competing against a full house. It is not worth the risk.

Your hand

The flop

Slim room for improvement

Even if the flop leaves you with a medium pair and a slim chance of a straight or flush with the turn and the river, you should still fold. In this hand, the flop gives you a pair of 9s, a possible flush (two clubs required), and a possible three of a kind (9s). If other players are betting, they are likely to have Aces and Jacks as hole cards and can probably beat you already. It is not worth risking that the turn and the river will give you the cards you need to compete.

Your hand

The flop

A good flop

If the flop does help your hand you should bet, but you should be aware of potential pitfalls before getting carried away with your hand. For example, consider the opening hand of a moderate pair, say 9s, where the flop gives you three of a kind. Depending on the other cards in the flop, your betting could be influenced either way.

Three of a kind: example 1

In this example, there is a chance that the flop has provided someone with a higher three of a kind (Aces or Queens), or that a player has at least paired with the chance of getting the higher-ranking three of a kind with the turn and the river.

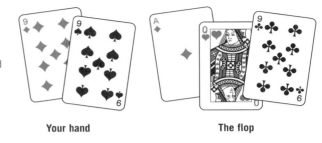

Your hand   **The flop**

Three of a kind: example 2

Here, your hand is likely to be the best at the table so far and it is worth betting. A higher-ranking three of a kind is unlikely, as is a flush, because nobody can be holding four of a suit yet.

Your hand   **The flop**

The potential combinations with the flop will be countless among your opponents and you can only use your judgement in knowing how to bet. It is essential to "read" the moves other players make and your position in relation to the dealer may be an advantage (see page 75).

The turn

The action tends not to change dramatically with the turn as, in many cases, the hands that are still in are not improved. Look out for a flop that contains two cards of the same suit and a turn that reveals a third: this may give an opponent a flush.

Suited cards

With two hearts in the flop and another in the turn, an opponent may be in with a good chance of completing a flush with his hole cards and the river.

The flop   **The turn**

The river

By the turn of the last community card, you either have a winning hand or you don't. Of course, there is always the chance that an opponent will find a flush or straight by the back door – that is, completing the hand unintentionally with favorable cards from the turn and the river – and this can radically change the outcome of the game.

A back-door win

Here, an opponent has a pair with an Ace kicker from the flop and may have hopes for three of a kind. Instead, he completes a straight by the back door.

The deal

The flop

The turn

The river

Bluffing

In **no-limit** games like this, in which the blind bets increase with each round, a player with a diminishing pile of chips is often **forced to bluff**. He does not have the luxury of waiting for a good hand to rebuild his pile, so has to stake everything on a bad hand. If he is called by an opponent who senses his predicament, he can hope to improve his hand only with the community cards. At the same time, once his pile starts to look vulnerable, opponents with more chips may try to bluff him out of the game, knowing that he will be reluctant to stake his few remaining chips on inferior hands. They have the luxury of being in a stronger position simply because they have more chips, not necessarily because of the cards they hold. This is one of the situations that makes Texas hold'em so fascinating: quite often, everything will depend on whether one player is bluffing or not and whether the other players can tell.

The following example shows how a bluff might work. Player 2 has made a 4,000-chip small blind, and player 3 has put in a big blind of 8,000 chips.

First betting interval

- Player 4 folds.
- Player 5 raises 10,000 chips.
- Player 1 folds, as does player 2.
- Player 3's pile is diminishing, and he sees this as the best time to bluff. He calls. There are now 40,000 chips in the pot.

Player 3 has the worst hand at this point and has a slim chance of winning the hand. His funds are shrinking and he needs to bluff to stay in the competition.

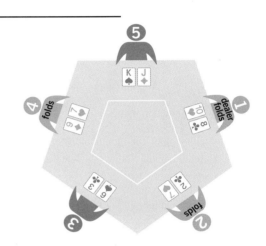

Second betting interval

- Player 3 bets 45,000 chips, taking the pot total to 85,000. If player 5 calls that will end the betting. The players would expose their cards, the dealer would deal the turn and the river and the best hand would win the pot. Player 3 needs to win to stay in the competition.
- The chances are that player 5 will fold. He will be intimidated by player 3's confidence and, although he has the better hand, he won't know this. He needs the turn and the river to strengthen his hand and may not feel betting further is worth the risk. If player 5 folds, player 3 wins the 85,000 chips of which 22,000 are winnings. He has retrieved his big blind and is in the competition for a few more rounds.

Player 3's success in the bluff is more likely with only one other player left in the game.

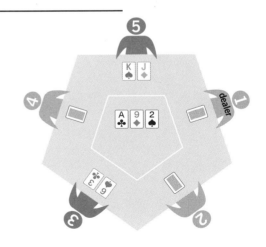

Omaha

A **relative newcomer** to the poker stable, Omaha is increasing rapidly in popularity as an alternative to stud poker (see page 88) and Texas hold'em (see page 68) in the casino. The game is similar to Texas hold'em, the main difference being that, in Omaha, each player receives **four** hole cards, of which he must use two, along with three cards from the board.

Example hand 1

- The player starts with promising hole cards: a pair of Jacks and a potential flush with the J/7 ♦.
- With the flop, his chances of the flush are improved with the 10 ♦, and there is even the chance of a straight flush, but this relies on the turn and the river to provide the 8/9 ♦. Other than that, he still has nothing stronger than the pair of Jacks in his hole cards.
- The turn and the river reveal the 5/4♣, giving the player a straight by the back door. Although a straight is likely to be the best hand that comes from this deal (a flush is impossible because no three community cards are suited), this player will probably lose to someone with a higher straight than his (for example, 10/9/8/7/6).

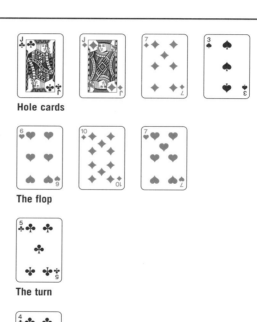

Hole cards

The flop

The turn

The river

Best hand: straight

Mixed fortunes

The chances of holding a better hand at the showdown are increased and this makes the game more complex. There are bound to be many different permutations and new players should familiarize themselves with this before betting for money. In the example shown opposite, the potential combinations are clear. Below, you can see how fortune can change as the game progresses.

Example hand 2

- The player has been dealt a frustrating hand. At first glance it looks as if he is well on the way to a high straight: A/K/Q/J/10. While it is not impossible, his position is not as strong as it looks, because he can use only two hole cards. This means he has to hope for the remaining three from the board.

- The flop gives him the Queen he needs, and the straight is still just possible. But the flop has given him something else, too. He now has a pair of Aces and a pair of 6s, which could lead to a full house.

- The turn confirms the full house. This player has a strong enough hand to win before the last card is shown. A fourth Ace would clinch it.

- The river brings a 5 – no use to the player, but he will be happy with a full house. Nobody else at the table can have a straight flush, as this requires three suited cards on the table. Nobody can have four of a kind with the Aces, because this player has the other Ace. The only hand that can beat him is a full house with Queens instead of 6s, requiring another player to hold the fourth Ace and a Queen among his four hole cards. This is possible, but the hand is worth a good bet.

Hole cards

The flop

The turn

The river

Best hand: full house

Basic play

Play follows the same form as Texas hold'em: A casino dealer shuffles and burns the top card before dealing four cards to each player. A button moves round the table, to the left with each deal, to indicate the notional dealer. Before play, an ante is put up or a small and big blind (see page 55).

There is a first betting interval once players have examined their hole cards. Then three community cards are dealt, face up, to the center of the table (the flop) and there is a second betting interval. A fourth card is dealt face up to the center of the table (the turn) followed by a third betting interval. A fifth and final card is dealt face up to the center of the table (the river) followed by the fourth and final betting interval, and then the showdown.

The following example shows each step of a given hand with five players. Player 1 is the notional dealer.

Stake limits

Ante: 5 chips.
Minimum bet or raise for intervals one and two: 1 chip.
Maximum bet or raise for intervals one and two: 3 chips.
Minimum bet or raise for intervals three and four: 3 chips.
Maximum bet or raise for intervals three and four: 10 chips.

First betting interval

- Player 2 speaks first and bets 2 chips. All other players call, making a pot of 15 chips.

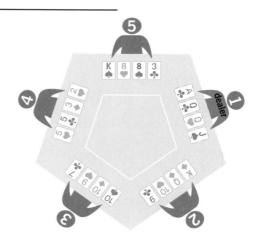

By the end of the first interval, all players remain in the game.

Second betting interval

- Player 2 has a potential straight, but he can use only two hole cards. He has other possible straights from the board and, perhaps, a straight flush, so he is still in a good position. He bets 2 chips.
- Player 3's hand has not improved much, as the 9 in the hole may not be of use. He has four chances of a straight, however, especially with an 8, so he calls.
- Player 4 is not helped by the flop. He folds.
- Player 5 is not helped by the flop, but has two 8s and three spades towards a flush: he calls.
- Player 1 has a pair of Queens – to his knowledge, the highest card in play – so he calls.

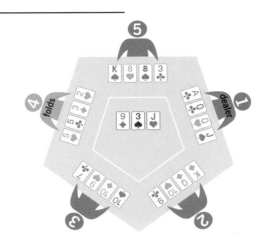

The flop has not been particularly helpful to any of the players. At the end of the second betting interval, there are 23 chips in the pot and four players remaining.

Third betting interval

- The turn reveals a 9♠, which has some influence on play.
- Player 2 has a strong hand. He has three 9s, and a good chance of scoring a full house on the river (needing a K, Q or 10). He also still has chances of a straight, so he bets the maximum of 10 chips.
- Player 3 is in a similar position. He also has three 9s and the chance of a full house with a 10 or 7 on the river. He calls.
- Player 5 has two pairs (9s and 8s) and can fill a full house with another 9 or 8. He also has four spades, and another on the river would give him a flush. He calls.
- Player 1 also has two pairs (Qs and 9s) and decides to call, in the hope that either would give him a good chance of winning. The pot is 63 chips.

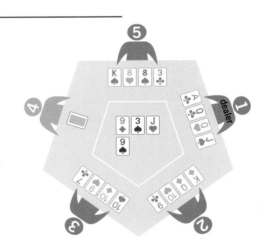

Fourth street improved most players' hands, but it is worth noting that all of them have the benefit of the pair of 9s on the board.

Who will win?

Before playing the hand out, consider who actually has the **best chance** of winning. With the benefit of knowing what all of the cards are, it is possible to see who has the greatest chance of winning the game. There are 28 cards left in the game.

- Player 2 has the best hand at the moment, with three 9s, a King, and a Jack.
- Player 1 can beat this with Q♠ (full house) or J♦/J♣ (three of a kind). This gives him three chances in 28.
- Player 3 can beat this with 10♣ (full house) or 7♠,♦, or ♥ (full house). He has four chances in 28.
- Player 5 can beat this with A, 6, 5, 4, or 2♠ (not Q♠, though, which wins for player 1, or 7♠, which wins for player 3) or 8♣ or♦. He has seven chances in 28.
- All other cards (14 in total) win for player 2, whether they improve his hand or not.

What are the odds?

Based on the example above, with 28 cards remaining, player 2 has an even chance of winning the pot; player 5's odds are 21 to 7 (3 to 1); player 3's are 24 to 4 (6 to 1); and player 3 has odds of 25 to 3 (more than 8 to 1).

Fourth betting interval

- The river reveals King♣. Player 2 continues to bet hard, knowing he has a strong hand with a full house. Again, he bets the maximum of 10 chips.
- Player 3 now has three 9s. He has staked a lot of money and, being a loose player (see page 63), he is willing to take the risk that this might be good enough to win the game.
- Players 5 and 1 fold.

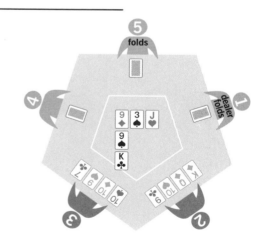

At the showdown, player 2 wins the pot, beating player 3's three of a kind with a full house. He wins a total of 83 chips.

Strategy

The permutations of potential winning hands with four hole cards are practically impossible to calculate, so, unlike Texas hold'em, no attempts have been made to give the opening hands any ranking. Instead, it takes familiarity with the game to know whether you have a good hand or not.

With this hand, you will have a range of possibilities, depending on the flop. Remember, you have to use two of your hole cards.

- Royal flush (requiring K, J, 10♥).
- Three or four Queens.
- Ace flush.
- Straights from different flops (A, K, J; K, J, 10; K, Q, J; K, J, 9; J, 9, 8).
- Two pairs (Aces/10s).

Look for suits and pairs

- The best hand before the flop is one with two cards of one suit and two of another, with all four cards connected or paired so that you have a range of potential alternatives with the flop. With this hand the board could produce a flush for either clubs or diamonds; or a straight using any two hole cards.

Be aware of limits to flushes

- There cannot be two flushes of different suits, because a flush requires three suited community cards, and this is only possible with one suit in any set of five cards.

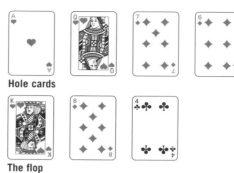

Hole cards

The flop

The turn

The river

Ignore three of a kind

- A pair in the hole cards is better than three of a kind, because you can use only two of the hole cards in your final hand. With this hand you can rule out a full house, 10s up, and four of a kind based on 10s, because you cannot use all three 10s. However, you could have a royal flush, in hearts, four of a kind in Aces, or a full house, Aces and 10s, which would require two Aces and a 10 in the community cards. As the community cards lie, however, the best hand here is three of a kind (Aces).

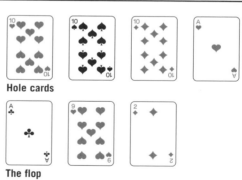

Hole cards

The flop

The turn

The river

Consider the board potential for others

- Always remember that the community cards are available to all players and may be put to better use with their hole cards than you can manage with yours. This hand looks promising with three Queens, but your best hand here is Q, Q, Q, 10, 7. Any other player can use the pair of Queens from the board and if another player holds the fourth Queen in the hole, he needs only one of his other three cards to be higher than 7 to have a better hand than you.

Hole cards

The flop

The turn

The river

Aggressive betting

For the best chances of winning, always look for your hole cards to work together, offering you a **range of alternatives** to pick just two cards from. If you are lucky enough to have two cards of one suit and two of another, and if among those cards you have a pair, then it is worth taking an aggressive betting policy. Forcing opponents to fold early, and collecting the pot, is generally a better policy than checking in the hope that other players will stake more chips. The more players who stay in the game as it progresses, the more cards become available, and the higher the chances of someone else getting a better hand than yours.

Stud poker

Stud poker, in particular seven-card stud, is one of the most played versions of the game in casinos across the globe. A game where the majority of the cards given to each player are dealt face up (up cards), there is great scope for strategy.

Stud poker is probably best played with six to eight players, although it can be played with as few as two. There is usually no ante (see page 55). Instead, table limits will have a fixed minimum bet but a maximum that increases as the game progresses. For example, a table may have a minimum bet of 1 chip for all betting intervals, a maximum of 2 chips for the first betting interval, and a maximum of 5 chips for the fourth betting interval. This upper limit may also come into play as soon as any player at the table has an "open pair" – that is, a pair showing in his face-up cards – which could happen as early as the second betting interval.

Other table limits may involve setting a new, raised maximum limit per betting interval, again with the provision that the upper limit comes into play once a player has an open pair. In some casinos the pot limit might be the maximum for a raise.

Betting protocol

As with other forms of poker played at the casino, a button passes around the table with each deal to indicate who is the notional dealer for that round. In each betting round, the player with the highest exposed hand always bets first. Should two players have the same hand – for example, if both have an Ace showing at the first betting interval – the player closer to the notional dealer's left starts the betting.

In addition to dealing the cards, the casino dealer will also direct play. With each betting round, he will announce which of the players should make the first bet – for example, he will point to the hand and say "Ace high" or "pair of 7s." When it comes to dealing the third and fourth up cards, the casino dealer will also point out the possible hand that can be made by each player, for example, "possible flush" or "possible straight."

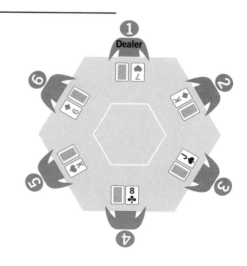

In the first betting interval the player with the highest card showing opens the betting. In this example, two players have Kings (2 and 5), and so the one nearest the dealer's left starts – that is, player 2.

Five-card stud

This is the simplest form of the game, played more usually in domestic situations than at a casino, but the basics are the foundation of seven-card stud. In five-card stud, each player is dealt five cards as play progresses, from which he must make the best poker hand possible. The players receive one card face down – **the hole card** – and the remaining four cards face up during a series of betting intervals.

Order of play

Hole card | **First betting interval** | **Second betting interval** | **Third betting interval** | **Fourth betting interval**

- The dealer shuffles the cards, cuts them, and then burns the top card. He deals one card face down to each player and a second card face up.
- On examination of these first two cards (the hole card is not revealed until the showdown), the player with the highest card showing must bet within the agreed limits. He cannot check or fold. Subsequent players then make their bets and each must fold, call, or raise. The betting continues around the table until all bets are equalized.
- A second face-up card is dealt to each player still in the game.
- There is a second betting interval. Again, the player with the highest hand so far is the one to bet first. In this, and subsequent betting intervals, he can check. Following players can check also, until a bet is made, after which they must fold, call, or raise.
- When all bets are equal, each player receives a third face-up card, and the third betting interval takes place.
- The players receive a fourth and final face-up card, after which the fourth betting interval takes place, followed by the showdown.

The showdown

If two or more players are still in the game by the end of the fourth betting interval, there is a showdown. Each player reveals his hole card, and the best hand wins. If all players except one have folded by the end of the fourth betting interval, the remaining player automatically wins the pot.

Example of a hand

The following demonstrates a hand of five-card stud with five players in the game. Betting limits are 1 chip for the first three betting intervals and 5 chips for the final betting interval. The betting limit increases to 5 chips once a player shows a pair. The shaded cards are the hole cards, known only to each of the players.

First betting interval

- Each player has been dealt one hole card and once face-up card. The player with the highest up card starts the betting – player 1 – who bets 1 chip on his pair of Queens, a strong opening hand.
- Players 2, 3, and 4 also have good opening hands, with a pair or potential flushes and straights, and each of them calls.
- Player 5 folds.

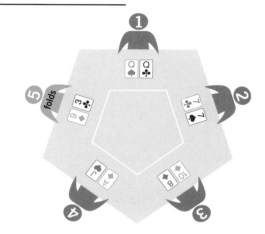

With four players left in the game, there are 4 chips in the pot.

Second betting interval

- Player 3 has the highest pair showing, and so bets first, and he thinks it is worth staying in the game. He stakes 5 chips – the new limit now that there is a pair on the table.
- Player 4 calls. He is still on track for a straight, but knows if that fails he still has a potential pair of Aces, Jacks, or 10s, which would beat player 3's hand.
- Player 1's hand has not improved, but his pair is the highest he can see. He does not want to draw attention to it quite yet, so he calls to stay in the game.
- Player 2 is in the strongest position with three of a kind, although nobody else knows this. He cannot be certain that player 3 does not have a third 8, but thinks it is worth the risk. He calls.

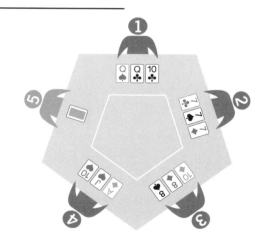

With all bets equal, there are still four players in the game and the pot is up to 24 chips.

Third betting interval

- With a pair of 10s showing, player 1 has the highest hand and is first to bet. He is intrigued that player 2 stayed in the last round with just a pair of 7s and thinks there is a chance his hole card is also a 7. But player 2 is not known for being a tight player, and may just be bluffing. With two high pairs, player 1 is prepared to take the gamble and bets 5 chips.
- Player 2 knows that player 1 is more likely to have two pairs at best, rather than three 10s. Player 2 calls.
- Player 3 folds.
- Player 4 has the highest hand that can be seen on the table, but senses that players 1 and 2 probably have stronger hands. From his up cards, it looks as if he could get a royal flush, and he thinks it is worth a bluff to stay in the game. He calls.

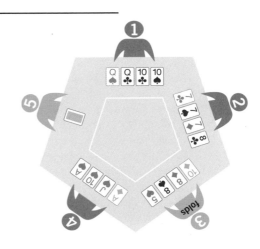

There are 39 chips in the pot and three players remain in the game.

Fourth betting interval

- Player 2 now has two pairs showing and is first to bet. He knows he has the best hand at the table – the best the other players can achieve is a triple – but does not want to scare off any more bets. He checks.
- His strategy works, and player 4 is convinced that player 2 has two pairs at best. This is the time to raise the stakes. He bets 5 chips.
- Player 1 knows he cannot compete. He can tell from the betting that players 2 and 4 have at least a triple each. He folds.
- Player 2 calls and raises 5 chips.
- Player 4 now realizes that player 2 probably has an 8 or 7 as his hole card, and therefore has a full house – but with a total of 54 chips in the pot he is willing to call for another 5 chips rather than risk losing the pot with a winning hand of three Aces.

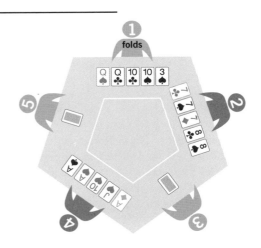

The showdown reveals player 2 to be the winner. He takes a pot of 59 chips.

Strategy

The safest strategy to adopt when playing five-card stud is not to bet at all if there is a better hand on the table than the one you hold, however many possibilities there might be with your hand. Tighter players will generally adhere to this rule: if another player has an Ace on the first interval, a tight player will fold unless he has an Ace in the hole. Looser players tend to chance their luck, but risk losing money from early betting intervals if they have to fold late in the game. In the previous example, player 2 had a strong hand from the beginning. His only competition was player 3, who could have had an 8 in the hole and, therefore, a higher triple. But player 2 knew this not to be the case when player 3 folded in the third betting interval. Player 4 should not have continued to bet past the second betting interval, but thought that player 2 was probably bluffing. By the end, player 4 had a hand that would have won on occasions, so his bluff almost paid off. Player 1 had good reason to feel he had a strong hand from the beginning – he always had the highest hand he could see on the table – but was let down by the last card.

Example of a hand

On examining their hands, the typical reactions of each player might be as follows:

- Player 1 would fold. All remaining players have a higher card than him on show and the odds on him winning are not good.
- Player 2 has an Ace in the hole and can see one other Ace on the table. A tight player might be deterred from betting against two players with higher cards than him showing. However, as his cards are both high and suited he would probably be tempted to aim for a flush – or at least bluff. A loose player would definitely take the risk.
- Player 3 has an Ace showing, but only a 4 in the hole. Nevertheless he is unlikely not to bet. He has the highest card on the table and only needs a pair of Aces to put him in the strongest position.
- Player 4, although he does not have an Ace, is likely to bet. There is only one other card on the table higher than his, and he has a chance of getting a high pair, three of a kind, or a straight. A loose player would not hesitate.
- Player 5 has a dilemma. He has the best hand on the table, but does not know. Even if he assumes that he is the only player with a pair, the chances of at least three other players making a higher pair from later deals is too great for a tight player. A loose player might chance getting a third 9 in the next round, but is likely to fold at that point.

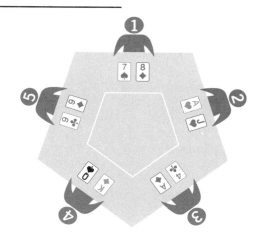

An example of a deal to show how players employ basic strategy when playing five-card stud. Their decisions will always be influenced by whether they tend to be tight or loose players.

Seven-card stud

Seven-card stud is the **favorite version** of poker for playing in the casino. Played in the same way as five-card stud, the major difference is that the players have **seven** cards from which to make the best-possible five-card poker hand. As such, there is much greater scope in this game for better hands and more betting. With potentially 49 cards in action should all players remain in the game for the showdown, this game in theory can be played by a maximum of seven players.

Order of play

First betting interval **Second betting interval** **Third betting interval** **Fourth betting interval** **Fifth betting interval**

- The dealer shuffles the cards, cuts them, and then burns the top card. He deals one card face down to each player, followed by a second. Then he deals a third card face up.
- On examination of these first three cards (the hole cards are not revealed until the showdown), the player with the highest card showing must bet within the agreed limits. He cannot check or fold. Subsequent players then make their bets and each must fold, call, or raise. The betting continues around the table until all bets are equalized.
- The casino dealer deals a second face-up card to each player still in the game.
- There is a second betting interval. Again, the player with the highest hand showing so far is the one to bet first. In this and subsequent betting intervals, this player has the option of checking. Following players can check also, until a bet is made, after which they must fold, call, or raise.
- When all bets are equal, each player receives a third face-up card, and the third betting interval takes place, followed by a fourth face-up card and the fourth betting interval.
- The players now receive their seventh card, this time face down, and there is a final betting interval, followed by the showdown.

Table limits

It is not common to have an ante in stud poker (see page 55) and most casinos tables will have limits to bets and raises, which could be:
- Each bet or raise could be limited to 1 or 2 chips.
- Each bet or raise could be limited to between 1 and 5 chips.
- There could be a limit on the first three betting intervals (by which time each player in the game has five cards) of, say 1 or 2 chips, with an increased upper limit for the last two betting intervals.
- The convention of raising the bet limit with an open pair (see five-card stud, page 88) is not usually used in seven-card stud.

Example of a hand

In this example of a hand of seven-card stud, there are five players in the game. The stakes are limited to 2 chips for the first two betting intervals and 5 chips for betting intervals three, four, and five.

First betting interval

- Player 5 has the highest up card and so bets first. He stakes 2 chips.
- Players 1, 2, 3, and 4 call.

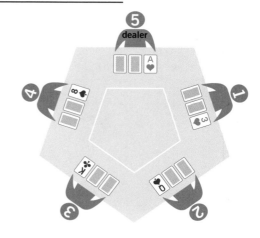

All players remain in the game and the pot is 10 chips.

Second betting interval

- Player 1 has a pair, and so the highest hand on view. He bets first, with 2 chips.
- Players 2, 3, and 4 call.
- Player 5 folds. Despite holding an Ace, he has four unrelated cards and sees no benefit in playing on.

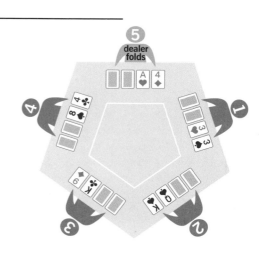

With four players still in the game, the pot stands at 18 chips.

Third betting interval

- With the next deal, player 1 still has the highest hand on the table with his pair. In fact, with the hole cards now revealed to us, we can see he has three of a kind. He bets 2 chips.
- Player 2 needs a Jack for a straight (none has shown so far) or two spades for a flush. The odds are against him, but he wants to stay in the game. He calls.
- Player 3 has two pairs, Kings up, and calls.
- Player 4 folds on a pair of 6s.

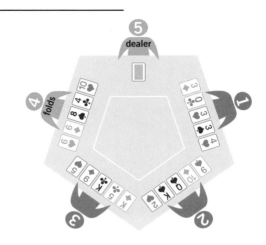

With three players left in the game, there are 24 chips in the pot.

Fourth betting interval

- Player 1 still has the highest hand, now with two pairs, and is to bet first. He has a full house and decides to bet the maximum of 5 chips. This will indicate to the other players that he has full house, but this does not worry him. The more cards they get, the more likely they are to get a full house, too, and his is easily beaten.
- Player 2 is certain he cannot win, and folds.
- Player 3 has three pairs and knows that he can win if he picks up a King, 9, or 5 with the final deal. Remembering the cards that he has seen face up so far tells him that there has been one King, but no 9s or 5s. Any one of five cards can win him the pot, unless player 1 has four of a kind. This leaves 28 cards out of the 33 he has not seen, so the odds of him winning are 28 to 5. He has to put 5 chips in to call and the pot stands at 29 chips – it is near enough an even bet for him. He calls.

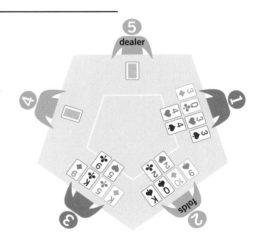

With players 1 and 3 remaining, the pot is 34 chips.

Fifth betting interval

- Both players receive their final cards and neither improves his hand. Both players check.
- At the showdown, player 1 wins with his full house, and takes the pot of 34 chips.

Strategy

When it comes to strategy in seven-card stud, the most important decision you make will be whether or not to stay in the game at the first betting interval. At this point you have two hole cards and an up card. In examining these cards, you should consider what kind of hand you are looking for, and should look at the other players' hands to see if any of the cards you might need has already been dealt. Even at this point, there are hands that are considered good and bad, and you should know what the chances of winning are with each of five combinations:

Good and bad hands

Three of a kind

Strategy
This is the best combination you can have, with chances of a full house and four of a kind. Stay in the game, but do not raise the stakes while betting keeps going. You can start to raise the stakes later in the game.

A pair with an odd card

Strategy
The pair should be either high – Jack or above – or, if smaller, should have a high odd card – Ace or King. Keep an eye on any matching cards that get dealt elsewhere, as they could spoil your chances of improving. Rarely continue beyond the fifth card without at least two pairs, and be wary of any pair on the table that is higher than yours.

Three of the same suit

Strategy
This has potential for a flush, but if the fourth and fifth cards are not of the same suit you should fold: your chances of getting two suited cards from the remaining deals are slim, even if there are not many showing on the table.

Three to a straight

Strategy
If you do not have four consecutive cards after the second betting interval, you should fold. Do not be tempted to go for a possible straight with gaps, as the chances of filling them are low.

High cards

Strategy
Two or three high cards, such as Ace, Queen, Jack or Ace, King, 6. But if the next card fails to fill a pair, you should fold. Four unrelated cards are likely to come to nothing.

Although these are good basic guidelines, you do not have to adhere to them strictly; use your intuition when it comes to playing on. As play progresses, new options may come to you and your hand may improve along different lines to those you expected.

Betting strategy
Players with strong opening hands – that is where both hole cards are promising for a winning hand – tend to bet moderately at first so that other players stay in the game. Once your up cards start to look strong, say you have two Aces showing, you could raise as a bluff, intimidating players into thinking you have three of a kind, especially if their hands are looking strong, too. Keeping an eye on the other players' hands is crucial. If they are betting strongly and you are fairly certain they have a better hand than you, you should fold.

Blackjack

Blackjack

Currently the most popular casino game in the US, blackjack is thought to be of French origin and to have derived from games such as "chemin de fer" (see page 23). The original game was called "vingt-et-un" (twenty-and-one) and was first played in French casinos in about 1700.

Although the game had migrated to the US by the early 1800s, it was not until a century later that it was introduced into the casino, and even then it was not met with enthusiasm. In order to entice gamblers to play, casino managers offered odds of 10 to 1 for players who scored 21 with the Ace ♠ and either of the two black Jacks in the pack. The odds did not stick (payout is now 3 to 2 for any hand with an Ace and 10-value card) but the game did, and this is how blackjack got its name.

Blackjack basics

Blackjack is a table game in which up to seven players face a dealer. Each player plays one-on-one with the dealer, and not with or against the other players at the table. The object of the game is to hold a hand of two or more cards that is higher than that of the dealer, but does not exceed a maximum score of 21. Players who win with a **"blackjack"** – that is, a two-card hand comprising an Ace and any 10-value card, making a total of 21 – are paid at odds of 3 to 2. All other winning hands are paid at even money.

A hand that scores 21 with two cards – an Ace and a 10-count – is called a "natural" or "blackjack" and it beats all other hands.

Card values

All cards have their **pip value**, except the Ace – which can count as 1 or 11 – and picture cards (King, Queen, Jack), which count as 10. The Ace, when held by a player, can count as 1 or 11 at his discretion, and he can change his mind any number of times during play, depending on his other cards. The dealer, however, always has to count an Ace as 11 if he has a card count of 17 or more: for example, an Ace and 6 must count as 17. The four suits are irrelevant in blackjack.

Table layout

The blackjack table is a simple, curved affair at which the dealer stands one side facing up to seven betting spots. Each player sits at the table with a betting square in front of him, and all bets must be placed here during play. Play always works from the dealer's left, and although one player's game has no influence on any of the other players, it is commonly felt that the last position before the dealer, known as third base, is a disadvantageous spot, and is avoided by a good number of experienced players.

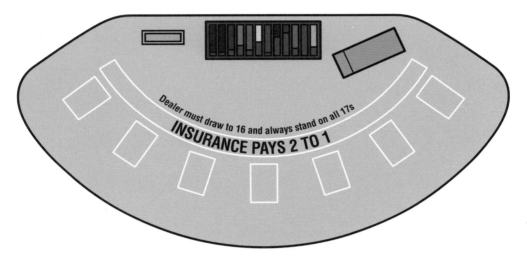

The currency slot is a hole into which the dealer drops the hard currency of players that is exchanged for chips at the start of play. The dealer cannot cash your chips at the end of the game: instead you need to go to the casino cash cage to exchange them.

The deal

Up to eight packs of cards are used in blackjack. They are shuffled by the dealer and cut by one of the players, who inserts an indicator card into the combined pack. The dealer completes the cut and places the cards face down in a dealing shoe, with the indicator card inserted a few cards up from the bottom – the cards below this will not be used. Before any cards are dealt, each player places a bet in the space before them, subject to the table minimum (see page 13).

The dealer burns the top card and, starting with the player on his left, he deals a card to each player, face up, and one to himself. He deals a second, face-up, card to all players, but this time his card is laid **face down**. This is known as the dealer's hole card and, by convention, is slipped under the dealer's up card. If the dealer's up card is an Ace or a 10-count, he looks at his second card. If he has a blackjack it is declared at this point and all bets are settled: any player who also has a blackjack ties with the dealer and retains his bet. All other players lose.

Profile of a blackjack player

The successful blackjack player is a dedicated gambler. Lured by the seemingly simple rules, he has learned the hard way that there is more to this game than pure chance. With several years' experience he now knows that sticking faithfully to the basic strategy is key to winning, and so plays his game accordingly. By taking advantage of the opportunity to double down and split pairs, he makes every effort to whittle down the house edge, and he is not always disappointed.

The play

If the dealer does not have a blackjack, his card remains face down and play continues, with the dealer attending to each player in turn starting from his left. Each player has one of four options.

Standing

If the player is satisfied with his two-card hand, he will **stand**.

Hitting

A player can **draw** another card, dealt face up, by saying "hit me" or scratching the table (see Blackjack etiquette, page 105). He can continue to draw cards until he is satisfied with his count. If his card count exceeds 21, he is **"bust"** and loses his stake to the dealer.

  Hit Hit

Splitting

If a player is dealt with two cards of the same rank, he can **"split the pair"** – make each card the first card of two separate hands – and place an equal bet on each hand. The dealer deals a second card to the first hand, and this is played out before the dealer deals a second card to the second hand. Again, some hands are considered better than others when it comes to splitting pairs (see opposite). Furthermore, there are a number of rules to consider when splitting pairs.

Splitting a pair

- The player splits a pair of 8s
  and receives a second card to
  each hand.

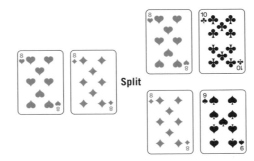

Split

Splitting Aces

- The player splits a pair of Aces.
  On receiving a third Ace, he
  can split again.

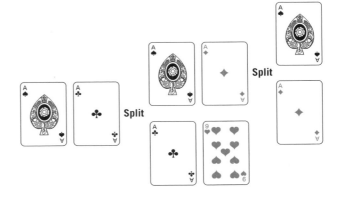

Split

Split

Scoring a blackjack

- The player scores a blackjack
  with a split Ace and wins the
  hand.

Split

- Should the second card in the split hand form a pair, the player
  can split again.
- If a player splits a pair of Aces, he is not allowed to draw a third
  card to either hand.
- If the player receives a third Ace, he may split again.
- Should a player score a blackjack with a split pair, he wins
  immediately, but is paid only at 1 to 1 and not 3 to 2.

Doubling down

If a player thinks he has a very good chance of winning, he can **"double down."** This means he places a second bet on his hand in return for just one more card. This third card is dealt face down and is left untouched until all other players' bets have been settled. Some hands are considered better than others when it comes to doubling down (see page 109).

Sample hand

The player has a soft 17 (see page 107) and decides to double down. His third card is left face down until all other hands are resolved.

  Double down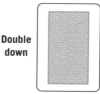

Surrender

It is also possible for a player to **surrender**, but there are two criteria:
- He must announce his intention to surrender at the start of his turn (not having hit, split or doubled down, for example).
- He can only surrender when the dealer has an Ace or 10-value card showing as his up card.

One of two things can happen if you surrender, depending on where you are playing: the dealer takes your cards and half of your bet there and then; or the dealer takes all of your bet, returning only half if he does not have a blackjack. The option to surrender is not available in all casinos.

Blackjack terminology

Blackjack A two-card hand that totals 21, comprising an Ace and a 10-count card. Also known as a natural.

Double down An option to make a second bet on the two-card hand by taking one more card.

Hit An option to receive another card (see page 102).

Insurance A side bet in which a player bets that the dealer has a blackjack, made when the dealer's up card is an Ace.

Natural Another term for a blackjack.

Split The option to take another card to each of the two original cards when a player has been dealt a pair.

Stand The decision not to take any additional cards.

Surrender The option to fold before taking any more cards, where the player forfeits half of his bet.

Winners and losers

In the early 1990s a group of maths students from the Massachusetts Institute of Technology (MIT) perfected a method of card counting that won them as much as $4 million in one year. Although a known concept, card counting was usually easy to detect because a player would bet consistently high stakes at a specific point in the game. The MIT students went undetected for at least two years because they worked as a team. In the simplest ruse, one member would take part in the action at a table, counting the cards and betting the minimum. When the cards began to get "hot" – that is when there was a greater percentage of high cards left in the pack (a disadvantage for the dealer) – the player betting the minimum would signal to a colleague, who would join the game and place large bets, until another signal told him to stop. The various team members adopted personas to suit their roles, variously as amateur better, high roller, and so on, which added to the deception.

Blackjack etiquette

In the interests of fair play, very few words are exchanged during blackjack. Instead, most instructions are given as sign language so that security cameras can observe all activity and there is no confusion about how each player wants to progress.

- In some casinos, and with single-deck games, the players' cards are dealt face down. If this is the case, you are allowed to pick up your cards, but should do so only with one hand and you must keep your cards above the table. In games where the cards are dealt face up, you must never touch the cards.
- If you want to stand, you wave your hand over the table, palm down.
- If you want to hit, you scratch the table with your hand, or scrape the table with the edge of your cards if you are allowed to hold them (see above).
- If you go bust, you lose automatically. If your cards are face down, you must immediately reveal your cards to the dealer.
- In the case of a "tie," the dealer knocks on the table, but leaves your bet where it is. You can leave it there, take it, or add to it for the next game as you wish.
- To double down or split a pair, simply slide another bet next to your original bet in the square in front of you. If your cards are concealed, turn them over as you do so. When splitting pairs, you have to match your original bet, while when doubling down, you can bet less than the original stake but not more.
- You should not look at your third card when doubling down until the end of play.
- The only verbal exchange you should have is when you want to surrender – in which case you announce the word instead of making any hand signals.

The dealer's hand

Once all players at the table have completed their hands, it is the dealer's turn to play out his hand. He turns over his hole card and, depending on his count, must follow strict rules of play:

- If the dealer has a hand of 16 or lower, he must draw, and continue to draw until his count is between 17 and 21, when he must stand.

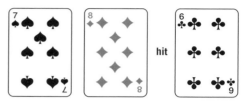

The dealer hits on 15 to score 21.

- If the dealer goes bust at this stage, all players still in the game win. (If you went bust before the dealer, you still lose.)

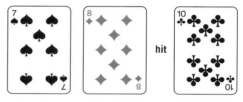

The dealer hits on 15 and busts with 25.

- The dealer must stand on 17 or above.

The dealer stands on 18.

- The dealer can count an Ace as one or 11, but only with a total of less than 17. If he holds and Ace and a 6, for example, he has to count the Ace as 11 and stand.

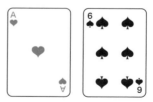

The dealer has to stand on soft 17.

Once the dealer stands, he pays all players with counts higher than his, and collects the stakes from those who are bust or have lower counts. If there is a tie, the player retains his stake.

Hard and soft hands

A hand can be described variously as **"hard"** or **"soft,"** depending on the cards you have. A soft hand is one in which an Ace can be used as either 1 or 11 without going bust. For example Ace and 7 can be counted either as 8 or 18. Should you be dealt an additional 10, the Ace has to count as 1 to prevent you going bust, so you have a hard hand with a count of 18. Any hand that does not contain an Ace is also a hard hand, because the pip count cannot change.

"Hard" 18

This is a hard 18, because the values of the cards can only be read one way: 10 and 8.

"Soft" 18

This is a soft 18, because the Ace can be read as 11 or 1.

"Hard" 18

This is a hard 18, because the Ace can now only be read as 1 without the player going bust.

Casino variations

A blackjack game follows the same rules in all casinos, although some casinos will have a few house rules of their own. These might include any of the following:

- The dealer draws on soft 17 (Ace/6).
- There is no insurance option (see page 108).
- The player's cards are dealt face down.
- Doubling down is restricted to certain hands (usually 9, 10, 11).
- Splitting pairs might be restricted.
- No option to surrender.

Playing to win

With the exception of poker, blackjack is the only game in the casino where a player's skill can influence the outcome of the game. In the simplest terms, success comes down to knowing when to hit, stand, double down, or split, and in the mid-1950s a group of mathematicians devised a **basic strategy** that has become the basis of many a winner's game plan today (see page 113).

In addition to applying this basic strategy, it pays to remember the odds in blackjack. The payout is simple: the dealer pays a player with a blackjack at odds of 3 to 2 while all other bets are settled at 1 to 1. Ties, including blackjack, are a standoff and the player retains his stake. It is possible to increase your bet during play, but only if you are splitting a pair or doubling down. In each case you should bet the same amount as your original stake (in fact, you have to if you split, while some casinos allow you to stake less when doubling down). When splitting and doubling down with successful hands, you stand the chance of reducing the house edge to less than 1 percent.

Finally, it cannot be stressed strongly enough that you do not have to score 21 in order to beat the dealer. There is no point risking going bust trying to get a score of 21, when the rules of the game are such that the dealer is likely to go bust during play anyway. You will lose your money if you go bust first.

Blackjack strategy

Fundamental to the strategy is the dealer's up card, and each player will play out his hand based on what he has. The rules can be organized in three categories, depending on the player's hand: **hard-hand strategy**, **soft-hand strategy**, and **splitting pairs**, as illustrated in the table opposite.

Insurance

If the dealer's up card is an Ace, all players have the option of insuring against him holding a blackjack. A player does this by putting up a premium of half his stake. If the dealer's hole card is a 10-count, he declares a blackjack. Any player that put up insurance is paid at odds of 2 to 1, and therefore retains his stake and premium – he neither wins nor loses the deal. If the dealer's up card is a 10-count, he also looks at the hole card. If he has a blackjack, all bets are settled, and insurance does not come into play.

Taking insurance is a side bet offering odds at 2 to 1 for what is essentially a 9 to 4 chance.

		Dealer's up card									
		2	3	4	5	6	7	8	9	10	A
Player's hard two-card total	9	DD	DD	DD	DD	DD	H	H	H	H	H
	10	DD	DD	DD	DD	DD	DD	DD	DD	H	H
	11	DD	DD	DD	DD	DD	DD	DD	DD	DD	DD
	12	H	H	S	S	S	H	H	H	H	H
	13	S	S	S	S	S	H	H	H	H	H
	14	S	S	S	S	S	H	H	H	H	H
	15	S	S	S	S	S	H	H	H	H	H
	16	S	S	S	S	S	H	H	H	S	S
	17	S	S	S	S	S	S	S	S	S	S
	18	S	S	S	S	S	S	S	S	S	S
	19	S	S	S	S	S	S	S	S	S	S
	20	S	S	S	S	S	S	S	S	S	S
Player's soft two-card total	13 (A/2)	H	H	H	H	DD	H	H	H	H	H
	14 (A/3)	H	H	H	H	DD	H	H	H	H	H
	15 (A/4)	H	H	H	H	DD	H	H	H	H	H
	16 (A/5)	H	H	H	H	DD	H	H	H	H	H
	17 (A/6)	DD	DD	DD	DD	DD	H	H	H	H	H
	18 (A/7)	S	S	S	S	S	S	H	H	H	H
	19 (A/8)	S	S	S	S	S	S	S	S	S	S
	20 (A/9)	S	S	S	S	S	S	S	S	S	S
Player's pair	2/2	SP	SP	SP	SP	SP	SP	X	X	X	X
	3/3	SP	SP	SP	SP	SP	SP	X	X	X	X
	4/4	X	X	X	X	X	X	X	X	X	X
	5/5	X	X	X	X	X	X	X	X	X	X
	6/6	SP	SP	SP	SP	SP	X	X	X	X	X
	7/7	SP	SP	SP	SP	SP	SP	X	X	X	X
	8/8	SP	SP	SP	SP	SP	SP	SP	X	X	SP
	9/9	SP	SP	SP	SP	SP	X	X	X	X	X
	10/10	X	X	X	X	X	X	X	X	X	X
	A/A	SP	SP	SP	SP	SP	SP	SP	SP	SP	SP

H = hit   DD = double down
S = stand   SP = split
                 X = do not split

Example of a hand

This illustration shows how one round of blackjack plays out, with seven players at the table. Each player has a stake of 5 chips – the minimum bet. The dealer's up card is 7, and the player's follow the above strategy:

Dealer's hand

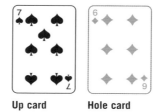

Up card   **Hole card**

Player 1 has hard 13. He hits with a 7, which takes his count to 20. He stands.

 Hit

Player 1: hard 13   **Count 20**

Player 2 has hard 17 and he stands.

 Stand

Player 2: hard 17

  Split

Player 3: pair of 8s   **Count 18**

Player 3 has a pair of 8s, which he splits. His first 8 gets a Queen and he stands on 18. The second 8 gets a 3. Player 3 hits again, with a Jack, and stands on 21.

Count 21

Player 4 has soft 17. He hits with a Jack, which keeps his count at 17. He stands.

  Hit

Player 4: soft 17   **Count 17**

Player 5 has soft 20 and he stands.

 Stand

Player 5: soft 20

Player 6 has hard 11 and doubles down, staking a further 5 chips, as any 10-count card would give him the total of 21. However, he gets a 6 for a total of 17, and since he cannot receive any further cards after doubling down, he stands.

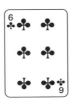 Double down

Player 6: hard 11   **Count 17**

Player 7 has hard 12. He hits with a 7, which takes his hand to 19 and he stands.

  Hit

Player 7: hard 12   **Count 19**

The dealer reveals his hole card – a 6. He hits with another 6, which takes his count to 19 – a good hand for the dealer. The dealer beats players 2, 4, and 6 outright. Player 6 doubled down, so the dealer takes 10 chips from him. He ties with player 7, who keeps his stake. Player 3 split his pair and won on one hand but lost on the other: the dealer takes the 5 chips for the losing hand, but has to pay 5 chips to the winning one. The dealer loses to players 1 and 5 and has to pay each 5 chips. By the end of play, the dealer is 10 chips up, players 1 and 5 are 5 chips up, players 3 and 7 stand still; players 2 and 4 are 5 chips down, and player 6 is 10 chips down. Using the above strategy, only three of the seven players lost money, despite this being a good hand for the dealer.

Blackjack derivatives

In recent years, casinos have introduced derivative blackjack games to the list of table games on offer. To some extent, these games aim to eliminate card counting and to increase the house edge. They have also been introduced to help maintain an amateur interest in the game, which has been seen to dwindle over the last decade. A few of the games are merely a ruse to make more money from the amateur and are best avoided.

Under/Over

In this version of the game you have the opportunity to bet on whether your next two-card hand will have a count of over 13 or under 13. There are two catches with this game: first, all Aces count as 1; second, if you have a count of exactly 13, the dealer wins.

Red or black

Here you can bet on whether the first-dealt card of your next hand will be red or black. So if you bet red, and the first card is red, you win. The catch here is that if the second card is also red you only tie.

Double exposure

In this game both of the dealer's cards are shown face up. This would seem an advantage, but there are a couple of catches: first, a blackjack is only paid out at even money; second, the dealer wins all ties. On both counts, you are worse off than playing the original game.

However, there are some derivatives that can be both entertaining and profitable for the experienced amateur, although in the case of Spanish 21, further reading on basic strategy is advised.

Multi-action blackjack

In this game you play out one hand, while the dealer plays out three hands, all using the same up card. You make a bet on any number of the three hands and each is counted separately.

Gambler beware

A number of professional gamblers use the strategy of card counting to increase their odds of winning. First introduced in the 1962 publication *Beat the Dealer* by Ed Thorp, the system involves counting the high cards as they appear on the table. In the most general terms, owing to the strict rules of the game, the dealer is better off with fewer high cards in the unused pack. This means a card counter can really play his luck if a high number remain. It certainly works in the long term but beware, as card counters are barred from the casino if they are discovered.

Tips for optimum success

In addition to the basic strategy, here are a few guidelines for success at blackjack, bearing in mind that casino rules can vary slightly.
- Always remember that the object of the game is to beat the dealer, and not necessarily to get as close a count to 21 as possible.
- Always try to play at tables where the dealer has to stand on 17 – in some casinos, he has an option to hit.
- Always try to play in single-deck games, or at least where there are no more than four packs of cards.
- Always try to play at tables where there are no restrictions on splitting and doubling down.

Spanish 21

This is a more complex game, where the basic rules of the game are extended and there are extra payouts for specific hands. The major differences are that you can double down on any number of cards – that is after hitting or splitting – and that you can surrender if you do not like your initial two-card hand, losing only half of your bet. Extra payouts include the following:
- A count of 21 using five cards pays 3 to 2.
- A count of 21 using six cards pays 2 to 1.
- A count of 21 using seven or more cards pays 3 to 1
- A three-card hand of unsuited 6, 7, 8 pays 3 to 2.
- A three-card hand of suited 6, 7, 8 pays 2 to 1.
- A three-card hand of 6, 7, 8 ♠ pays 3 to 1.
- Unsuited 7, 7, 7 pays 3 to 2.
- Suited 7, 7, 7 pays 2 to 1.
- Three 7s ♠ pays 3 to 1.

Other games

Slot machines

Fruit machines, one-armed bandits, and slots are all common names for the various slot machines available to today's gamblers. In the 50 or so years since they were first introduced to the casino, they have rapidly become **the most popular attraction** there and account for as much as two-thirds of many a casino's revenue.

They have come a long way since American inventor Charles Fey produced the "Liberty Bell" in 1898, however. Considered the forerunner of the modern machine, the Liberty Bell operated on a simple three-reel mechanism. Although today's machines are more complex – sometimes with as many as five reels and multiple pay lines – and are computer-operated, the principle is primarily unchanged.

The basics

In the simplest terms, a slot machine has a number of reels, each displaying a range of symbols. Instructions on the front of the machine tell you how much money to play and display a number of winning combinations together with their payouts. The reels spin and, if you have a winning combination of symbols on the pay line when the reels come to rest, you win.

Today's slots machines present all manner of playing options. You can play machines with fixed payouts or opt for one that offers a progressive payout, based on a percentage of the money you have

Payout

Every slot machine has been preprogrammed to allow a certain number of wins, based on a percentage of the money paid into it. Different countries, even different states within the US, have a legal minimum that casinos must comply with, and most machines fall somewhere between a 70 and 95 per cent payout. Machines with a higher payout percentage are referred to as "loose" and those with a lower payout percentage as "tight." The program is determined by a random number generator (RNG), which means there is no way of determining when a payout is due: two jackpots may follow in succession on one occasion, while there may be days between wins on another.

played so far. You can even play machines that are linked to other machines – sometimes in more than one casino – where the potential jackpot can be literally millions for just one player. The machines can operate on a one-, two-, or three-coin maximum (or more) and offer proportional payouts, multiple pay lines, or bonus options depending on how much you put in.

Slot-machine strategy

Much of the appeal of the slot machine lies in the fact that gamblers play alone at their own pace, and require very little skill. It is a good idea to watch the slot-machine action on the casino floor before getting started, as you will quickly find out which machines are paying out more often than others. Make sure you understand the type of machine you are playing on, how it operates, and what the payout system is. Be wary of machines with maximum-coin functions. The payouts can be bigger, but they are activated progressively and you may miss out with them if you are not prepared to play up to the maximum.

Video Poker

First seen in the late 1970s, video poker and its various spin-offs has grown in popularity and is now a favorite among slot-machine regulars. Based on a simple 5-card draw, the game offers the poker enthusiast a chance to test his skills without having to experience the tension and pressure of traditional backroom poker.

Having inserted a coin or credit to start a game, the player is dealt five cards from a virtual pack. On examining his cards, he has the option of discarding any number of cards in favor for new ones from the same deck. He can replace each card only once. Depending on the winning hands shown on the front of the machine, the player receives a payout. Winning hands are ranked in the same order as those for traditional poker, and most machines operate on a minimum payout for a pair of Jacks. Anything lower loses.

Some versions of video poker include the use of wild cards – usually the 2 (deuce), or offer multiplay options to the gambler. With the latter, the gambler is dealt a number of hands – 3, 5, or 10, for example – each from a different virtual pack of cards. He then plays each hand out in turn.

Keno

With the promise of potentially massive payouts on small wagers, keno has become a popular side attraction for casino gamblers over the years. Brought to the US by Chinese immigrants building the transcontinental railway, this game is a form of lottery. Every casino will have a keno brochure listing information on minimum bets, payouts, and the various tickets you can play.

The basics

The standard game involves a house draw of 20 numbers from a possible 80. Players buy a ticket on which they highlight anything from 1 to 15 numbers. Depending on how many numbers they choose and how many match those picked out by the casino, players stand to win thousands on just one game. High payouts come at a price: the house edge in keno is anything from 25 to 40 per cent.

The ticket

Each keno ticket has a grid marked with numbers from 1 to 80. Once you have made your selection, using the keno crayon provided, your ticket is validated by a keno clerk. He will keep your ticket – marked with the value of the bet you want to make and the type of

A standard keno ticket marked up for a straight eight-spot game.

game being played (see below) – and will issue you with a duplicate. Once marked, the numbers are referred to as "spots" and if you choose, say, eight numbers, you are playing an eight-spot game. Should any of your numbers come up, you need to present your ticket in order to claim a win.

The draw

In most casinos, keno games tend to run every five to ten minutes throughout the day. The winning numbers are usually picked at random by a computer, although some casinos still operate the game with ping-pong-type balls in a transparent plastic sphere. Every casino will have a designated keno lounge where players can follow the action at their leisure, but the results are also generally posted on television monitors throughout the casino. You can use keno "runners" to collect your marked-up tickets or bring you your winnings – just beware that you run the risk of forfeiting your takings if they are not collected before the start of the next game.

Much like bingo, you win if you match the numbers from the draw. Unlike bingo, however, the payout improves depending on the winning numbers as a percentage of your original selection.

The game described above is referred to as straight keno – that is, you mark one ticket with a selection of numbers and place one bet on those numbers turning up in the next game. If you have several matches, you may be eligible for a win, and you must claim that win before the next game starts. Payouts vary from casino to casino, but the following offers an example for straight keno: if you pick five numbers, you usually have to match three of them to be able to claim a win, for which the odds are usually 3 to 1. With four matching numbers, you would be paid back at odds closer to 25 to 1, and with five, the odds could be close to 300 to 1.

Keno variations

In addition to the straight game, casinos offer other ways to play keno.
- **Multi-race keno** In this version, players have the option of playing the same keno ticket in a set number of games. Once the given series of games has been played out – say 20 – you return your ticket to the keno clerk to check them for winning games.
- **Way tickets** This version allows the player to choose several groups of numbers, each containing the same number of digits – say three. One winning number in each group constitutes a win for that ticket.

Casino poker

Table variations of poker are relative newcomers to the casino, arising largely from the "supercasino" explosion in Las Vegas of the 1990s. They were introduced by casino managers exploiting the American love of the game and the fact that amateur gamblers were often intimidated by the more traditional backroom games like Texas hold'em (see pages 68–79).

The basics

Although these poker variations may differ in the way they are played, they do share a number of common factors. For example, they are all played on a table that is similar to the blackjack table (see page 101), at which up to seven players can sit; with the exception of let it ride (see below), each player plays one-on-one against the dealer, not against the other players; each game uses a standard pack of 52 cards; and winning hands follow the ranks of traditional poker (see pages 52–53).

Let it ride

This is a game in which players simply have to make the best-possible poker hand from three cards dealt to them, plus two community cards available to all players (note that players do not play against the dealer in this game). Each player has three betting circles in which he places three identical bets at the beginning of the game. He then receives his three cards, face down, while two community cards are placed, face down, at the center of the table. Having looked at his first three cards, each player has the option to retrieve his first bet if the hand looks weak. He does this by scratching the table, and the dealer returns the bet. If the player has a good hand (see below), he leaves the bet where it is – that is, he **"lets it ride."**

Let it ride payout

Royal flush 1,000 to 1
Straight flush 200 to 1
Four of a kind 50 to 1
Full house 11 to 1
Flush 8 to 1

Straight 5 to 1
Three of a kind 3 to 1
Two pairs 2 to 1
Pair of 10s or better 1 to 1

The dealer now reveals the first community card and each player examines his hand once more. This time he has the option of retrieving his second bet or letting it ride. Finally, the dealer reveals the second community card and the player makes the best poker hand from the five cards available to him. He cannot retrieve his third bet. The dealer pays the bets on each winning hand according to the payout table below – each hand must have a pair of 10s or better to qualify.

The house edge for let it ride can be as low as 3.5 percent, but you need to play basic strategy in order to benefit from this.
- Retrieve your first bet unless you have a pair of 10s or better; three of a kind; a three-card straight; or a three-card flush.
- Retrieve your second bet unless you have a pair of 10s or better; three or four of a kind; a four-card straight; or a four-card flush.

Example of a hand

- The player has a pair of Jacks, so lets his first bet ride.
- He gains nothing from the first commmunity card so retrieves his second bet. He has to let his third bet ride.
- The second community card gives the player two pairs.
- His bet of 10 chips wins him 20 (2 to 1, see table on page 120).

Player's hand

Three betting spots, each with a 5-chip stake

1st community card

2nd community card

Caribbean stud

To participate in a game of Caribbean stud each player first puts up an **ante** of the table minimum. He is then dealt five cards face down. The dealer includes himself in the deal, with his last card dealt face up. Each player plays one-on-one against the dealer and the best poker hand wins. Depending on the dealer's up card, the player has the option to surrender his hand at this point – thereby losing his ante – or to play out the hand. Should he play on, he places another bet on the table, which must be twice the value of his ante.

Play

Once all players have made their decisions, play continues with the dealer revealing his cards with the following possible outcomes.

- The dealer's hand must contain at least an Ace and a King for him to **"qualify"** and continue the game. If not, the dealer must fold and the players still in the game win on their antes – paid at even money – and tie on their second bet. The game ends here.
- If the dealer's hand contains at least an Ace and a King, he goes on to form the best possible poker hand with his five cards. If you have a better poker hand than the dealer, you win. The ante bet is paid at even money, while the second bet is paid at the odds determined by your hand (see below).
- If the dealer has a better hand than you, you lose both bets.

Strategy

Caribbean stud has a house edge of approximately 5 percent. When deciding whether or not to play your hand, a reasonable strategy is to play if you have at least an Ace and a King.

Payout odds

A winning hand will earn the following odds on your second bet, depending on the cards you have. They may vary from casino to casino.

Poker hand	Odds	Poker hand	Odds
Royal flush	100 to 1	Straight	4 to 1
Straight flush	50 to 1	Three of a kind	3 to 1
Four of a kind	20 to 1	Two pairs	2 to 1
Full house	7 to 1	One pair or less	1 to 1
Flush	5 to 1		

Progressive payouts

Players participating in this game have the opportunity to make a side bet on their hand, which could potentially bring them a big win on a **progressive jackpot** (see table below). The side bet must be placed at the same time as the ante – that is, before any cards are dealt. Should the dealer fail to qualify you must declare a progressive jackpot hand before the cards are removed for the next game. There is rarely a win for a hand lower than a flush and if two or more players have the same hand, they split the payout. If you look at the approximate odds on winning the various payouts, it is easy to see that this is not a good bet.

Typical progressive jackpot payouts

Poker hand	Odds	Payout
Royal flush	650,000 to 1	100 percent of jackpot
Straight flush	65,000 to 1	10 percent of jackpot
Four of a kind	4,000 to 1	100 chips
Full house	700 to 1	75 chips
Flush	500 to 1	50 chips

Examples of a dealer's hand

Dealer's hand fails to qualify

A qualifying dealer's hand

Three-card poker

This three-card version of poker was first introduced into casinos in Great Britain in 1995. Since then it has also been introduced to the US and is currently played avidly across the globe.

The game has two stages and each can be considered a game in its own right. The first stage is **"pair plus,"** where the player bets that his three-card hand will contain a pair or better. The second stage is **"ante/play,"** where the player bets that his three-card hand will beat the dealer's hand. Most casinos allow players to bet on either stage or to bet on both at the same time.

Play

Before any cards are dealt, each player must decide whether he is going to bet on one or both aspects of the game, and place pair-plus and ante bets accordingly. He can stake a different amount for each bet within the table limits. The dealer deals three cards, face down, to each player and the same to himself. If a player is betting on the ante/play stage of the game, he must examine his cards and now has the option to fold or play. Should he play, he places his "play" bet on the table, which must equal his ante.

Once all players have made their decisions, play continues and the dealer reveals his cards with the following possible outcomes.
- The dealer's hand must contain at least a Queen for him to **"qualify"** and continue the game. If not, the dealer must fold and all players still in the game win on their antes – paid at even money – and tie on their play bet.
- If the dealer's hand contains at least a Queen, he plays his hand against that of each player. If you have a better hand than the dealer, you win both bets – paid at even money.
- If the dealer has a better hand than you, you lose both bets.
- A bonus is paid to all players who have a straight (1 to 1); three of a kind (4 to 1) or a straight flush (5 to 1). This "ante bonus" is paid out irrespective of whether the player wins or loses against the dealer.

Pair plus

With the ante/play stage of the game complete, the dealer now turns to players who made a pair-plus bet, and pays them accordingly. (Note that the ranks deviate from traditional poker because some are more difficult to achieve than others – three of a kind is harder to achieve than a straight or a flush, for example, and a straight is harder to achieve than a flush.)
- Straight flush: 40 to 1
- Three of a kind: 30 to 1

- Straight: 6 to 1
- Flush: 4 to 1
- Pair: 1 to 1

Example of a hand

The following is a straightforward example of a hand where the player has bet a
1-chip pair plus, a 2-chip ante, and a 2-chip play. He has a straight, while the
dealer has a Queen-high flush.

- The player's hand beats the dealer's hand and the player wins even money on his ante and play bets (4 chips).
- The player's hand qualifies for the ante bonus, paid at even money for a straight (2 chips).
- The player also wins his pair-plus bet, which is paid at 6 to 1 for a straight (6 chips).
- The player bet 5 chips and won 12 altogether.

Player's hand

Dealer's hand

Strategy
The house edge is 3.5 percent if you follow basic strategy, which is
to fold on anything less than Queen high.

Pai gow

Taking elements from an ancient Chinese game of dominoes and poker, pai gow poker is played **one-on-one** against the casino dealer. The game uses a standard pack of 52 cards, plus a Joker, which can be used as an Ace or to complete a straight, a flush, or a straight flush. The object of the game is to complete two hands from seven cards, both of which must beat the dealer's hand for a win.

Play

Each player places a bet in his own betting circle and the dealer then rolls a dice to determine who is dealt cards first. With a hand of seven cards, each player must make a five-card hand and a two-card hand. The relative values of the five-card hands are the same as in poker, with one exception: A/2/3/4/5 is the second highest type of straight or straight flush, ranking between A/K/Q/J/10 and K/Q/J/10/9. Five aces is the highest hand (made using the Joker) and beats a straight flush. The best two-card hand is a pair. The five-card hand always has to be higher than the two-card hand: if the two-card hand is a pair of 6s, for example, then the five-card hand must have a pair of 7s or better.

The outcome of each hand is as follows:
- The player wins if both hands beat those of the dealer. He is paid even money, minus a 5 percent commission to the casino.
- If the dealer wins both hands, the player loses his stake.
- If the player wins on one hand but loses on the other, it is a tie and no money changes hands.
- The dealer wins a tie.

Player banker

While the casino dealer usually plays out the first round or so of this game, it is customary for the position to rotate around the table, although there is no obligation for anyone to take on the role. In such a game, the remaining players play against the new banker, and not the casino. He pays all winning hands and collects any bets from those that lose. He also wins all ties. The casino's 5 percent commission on winning hands is not affected.

Gambler beware

Each player is responsible for arranging his own seven cards into two hands and he must ensure that the five-card hand is higher ranking than the two-card hand. If he fails to do this, his hand is considered "foul" and the player loses automatically.

Basic strategy

As in blackjack (see pages 100–113), pai gow poker has guidelines for basic strategy that could bring the house edge down to 2.5 percent.

Example of a hand

Player's hand

Best possible arrangement of cards into
A: a group of two
B: a group of five

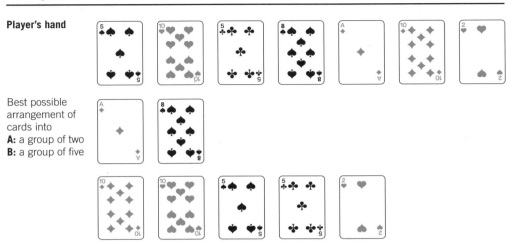

Reducing the house edge

Your Hand	Two-card strategy	Five-card strategy
Nothing	Use the second- and third-highest card	Use the highest card
One pair	Use the two highest single cards	Use the pair
Two pairs with an Ace	Use the Ace	Use both pairs
Two pairs	Use the low pair	Use the high pair
Three pairs	Use the highest pair	Use the second and third highest pairs
Five-card straight	Use the two odd cards	Use the straight
Six-card straight	Use the two highest cards that you can	Use the remaining straight
Flush	Use the highest cards you can without breaking up the flush	Use the flush
Full house	Use the pair	Use the three of a kind

Gambling at home

Gambling at home

For those who have neither the time nor the inclination to go the distance to visit a casino, there are, of course, plenty of opportunities for gambling at home. There is no shortage of professional gaming equipment available to devotees of any casino game (see page 134), and you can quite easily, and successfully, organize a casino night, or even weekend at home.

And if that does not appeal, there is, of course, the Internet. Every game that is available to the casino gambler is also on offer online. There are literally countless highly effective gaming websites featuring poker, blackjack, craps, roulette, baccarat, and more that you can play in the comfort of your own home.

Online basics

In order to play online, you need to fulfill four essential criteria:
- The first is to make sure you are legally allowed to gamble online. Many countries and states prohibit gaming, in which case you risk prosecution.
- The second is that you have a working computer with a compatible operating system (primarily Microsoft Windows) and a high-speed Internet connection.
- The third is that you experiment with various software programs on a trial-run basis before playing any game for money: all reputable online casinos will allow you to do this – in some cases indefinitely.
- Finally, you will need to register with the online casino and set up a separate bank account through which you can deposit money and withdraw money from the casino as you play.

What to play?

You should approach gambling on the Internet in exactly the same way as you would playing at the casino. Decide on a game that suits you and your gambling style: are you looking for a game of pure chance or do you want to pit your skill and instincts against like-minded opponents? In addition to the traditional table games, you can play slot machines, keno, and the many variations of traditional games, from European roulette to pai gow poker. In many cases the graphics are so realistic that you can get a taste of the casino vibe.

Spoiled for choice?

If this is an option that appeals to you, make sure you do some homework first: not all gaming websites may be what they seem. Gambling online involves divulging personal bank details and parting with money – so make sure the website you choose is legitimate.

Choosing where to play online is possibly the hardest decision many Internet gamblers face. There are hundreds of thousands of websites and little way of making true comparisons between them. Gaming magazines and online search engines can help narrow down the field, but here is a list of criteria to help decide whether a website is a) reputable and b) safe. All of the following information should be readily available from various menus on a given website's homepage.

- Is the website licensed to operate casino games?
- Does the website operate using licensed software?
- Can you preview any one of the games before downloading the software?
- Can you download the software for a free trial before committing financially?
- Is the website's payout schedule reviewed regularly by an independent auditor?
- Does the website provide clear instructions for their banking requirements?
- Are the banking requirements secure?
- Will you have access to the records of all financial transactions you make with the casino?
- Will you have access to your full gaming history with the website?
- Does the website offer around-the-clock customer service?
- Does the website offer advice on sensible gambling?

In addition to fulfilling the above criteria, there will doubtless be various bonus and loyalty schemes to consider.

Online poker

Poker far outstrips any other game played on the Internet – some reports have suggested that there are as many as 100,000 US players online at any one time during peak playing times. There are numerous websites offering players all variations of the game, including Texas hold'em, Omaha, and seven-card stud – all of which are featured in Chapter 4. Players will also find the opportunity to play more recent casino poker variations, such as Caribbean stud, let it ride, and three-card poker (see Chapter 6).

The rules for playing these games are the same as those in a casino, although there are a few significant differences.

1 Primarily, you are playing on your own at home and not seated around a table with your fellow players. This means that you cannot benefit from watching your opponents' behavior during play. Although this may be seen as a disadvantage, it also means that you cannot give anything away either.

2 Instead of having to make mental notes about an opponent's performance, many poker websites allow you to enter, digitally, anything you might notice about a player during the game. This could include betting patterns, number of wins/losses, and so on.

3 Online poker tends to be a faster game than games played in the casino. The average speed of play on the Internet is some 60 hands per hour, compared with about 30 hands in the casino. One reason for this is that the cards are shuffled and dealt instantly online, taking no time at all. The speed of the game is increased further with auto-action buttons, which allows a player to determine his action before his turn.

4 An online player can take part in more than one game at any one time – joining the action at a number of tables. There is often an option to "sit in" – that is, to join the table and observe the action, getting a feel for the game before starting to play.

Self-analysis

One of the bonuses of playing virtual poker is that you can access digital records of your own gaming history with that website, making it possible to analyze your own poker play as well. You can search through games and their results, comparing the data for totals of winnings and losses, but also for general statistics about your play. This means you can detect short-term strengths and weaknesses that might help to improve your game in the long run.

Pros and cons of virtual versus real casino

Virtual casino	Real casino
Despite the high quality of many websites, it is impossible to create a real casino atmosphere.	Real casinos have an undeniable buzz that many would say is an integral part of creating the right gambling vibe.
Internet games often progress at an increased pace and can leave a player feeling that he is simply "going through the motions" rather than taking part in what should be an enjoyable pastime.	Although casino players are not encouraged to procrastinate – some casinos impose a time limit on each player's turn – there is nevertheless a slower pace, which enhances the overall enjoyment of playing cards to make money.
There is currently no standard legislation monitoring virtual casino activity.	Real casinos have to comply with state legislation.
Apart from the equipment and telephone line, costs involved in participation are minimal.	Gambling at a casino incurs significant additional costs, including travel, accommodation, and subsistence.
It provides an opportunity to "meet" fellow enthusiasts from all walks of life and around the world.	"Socializing" is restricted to those there at the time, and many casinos across the world have strict entrance requirements.
There is a higher risk of foul play, since there can be no guarantee that games are not "fixed" somehow for you to lose.	Stringent casino training for staff and conventions for clients limit the likelihood of foul play.
All results are generated by a computer using a random number generator (RNG). This somehow reduces the element of "chance" and "luck" in a game on the Internet.	Every game in the casino has a very real element of chance or luck – one of the most alluring aspects of playing for any gambler.

Poker explosion

The beginning of the 21st century witnessed an explosion in the interest in poker on an unprecedented scale, and this can be credited to some extent to the broadcasting of such events as the World Series of Poker (WSOP) and the World Poker Tour (WPT) on television in both the US and UK. Coupled with the rising fortunes of the world's top poker site, Party Poker, and the growing subscribers to online gambling, Texas hold'em in particular has gripped the world and shows no sign of abating.

Home casino

As mentioned previously, there is no end to the **gaming-related merchandise** that you can buy for playing casino games at home, and any one of the games featured in this book could be the focus of an entertaining evening in with friends. There are tables for craps, roulette, and blackjack, all complete with betting layouts, and professional chips and dice. Card players will find all manner of gadgets, from automatic card shufflers to casino-standard card shoes, and poker fanatics can even buy personalized chips and a dealer button. For an event with professional flair, it is possible to hire all of the relevant equipment, complete with catering and professional croupiers.

If you do intend to play casino games at home – with friends or colleagues – for money, it is important to guarantee that the evening is entertaining for everybody concerned. Anyone who has played at the casino, or remembers a particularly exciting game of poker at home, will know that winning and losing any sum of money can bring out strong emotions. In order to make sure that things do not get out of hand, it is sensible to take a few precautions.

- Establish a maximum period of play – say two hours. This will help players to have a sense of how long their money has to last, and will provide a cut-off point to prevent anyone gambling everything.
- Have sensible table limits: for example, one unit per bet with a five-unit maximum.
- Do not exceed the maximum number of players for any one game.
- With the exception of poker, if you do not hire croupiers, aim to have a non-player to run each game in order to avoid disputes between betters.
- Keep an eye on drinking. Casino nights are great fun and it is easy to be buoyed up by a win and knocked down by a loss. Alcohol and gambling do not mix.

Home rules and conventions

The majority of casino games can be played at home with little or no variation. A roulette wheel will come complete with the betting layout, chips, and a set of rules to follow, as will a craps table. In the case of poker, however, the situation is different, because in-house staff are responsible for shuffling and dealing the cards at the casino. They will also direct the progress of play. Dedicated poker players might like to observe the following conventions when setting up a poker game at home:

Players

You should decide on the number players you want in on the game before play starts. Although players can join the game once it has started – say, if someone else drops out – you should not exceed the maximum. You should also establish a time limit at which point play will end. Anyone joining the game during play is bound by this time limit, although any player can leave the game before the limit is reached.

Banker

One player needs to be selected as the banker. He is in charge of all of the chips and issues them to players, including those to himself, at their cash value. He also converts the chips into cash for players as they leave the game.

Seating

The banker has the first choice of seat and other players have the choice thereafter. If there is a dispute, the cards are shuffled by an agreed player and cut by another. The banker then deals a card to all the remaining players, face up. The player dealt the highest card (Ace) has the first choice of seat, followed by the player with the next highest, and so on. Players can change seats at any time after one hour of play and again after each subsequent hour of play.

Sequence of play

In poker everything passes to the left. The dealer deals the cards clockwise, one at a time, to all the players, beginning with the player to his left. The turn to bet passes from player to player to the left and when each hand is over, the player to the left of the previous dealer deals. Once everyone is seated, the first dealer is chosen in the same way that the seating was chosen (see above), except that the banker includes himself this time.

The ante

To make the game more rewarding financially for the winner, a number of chips are put into the pot before each deal – usually 1 chip per player. This is known as the "ante." Most commonly, each player puts 1 chip in before the deal. For convenience, sometimes the dealer puts in for all players – for example, if there were eight players, he would put in 8 chips. After eight deals, each player's contribution in antes is equal. The ante is placed in the center of the table and is usually kept separate from the stakes each player bets during the deal, as this ensures that the amount of each player's bet can easily be seen. The winner takes the ante and the bets at the end of each deal.

Shuffling and dealing

Before each deal, the cards must be shuffled at least three times. Any player may ask to shuffle, but the dealer always shuffles last. A good basic shuffle is to hold the pack of cards, face down, between the thumb and fingers of your left hand. Lift the majority of the pack with your right hand and use your left thumb to slide six to twelve cards from the top and onto the pile in your left hand. Repeat this process until all the cards are in the left hand, and start again.

After the shuffle, the dealer places the pack in front of the player to his right, who cuts the pack: he lifts a number of cards from the top of the pack, puts them down on the table, and then places the bottom section of the pack on top. Both piles must contain at least five cards.

The cards return to the dealer, who burns the top card by placing it face down on the table. This is the start of what will become the discard pile as the game progresses. The dealer then deals the cards one at a time to each player, including himself, beginning with the player to his left.

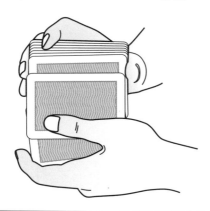

Wild cards

By mutual agreement, any card or cards in the pack may be designated "wild." The holder of the wild card may use it to represent any card he wishes. If he has a pair of Kings and a pair of 4s, a player can use the wild card to make a full house. (He cannot use it to duplicate a card that he already holds, that is, if he has all four Aces, he cannot use the wild card to give him a fifth.)

Traditionally, the most common way to introduce a wild card was by using the Joker, but now it is more usual to specify one whole rank as wild, most commonly the 2s (Deuces). The black Deuces are usually used if only two wild cards are wanted.

Draw Poker

One of the most popular versions of poker played at home is **draw poker**. Played following the basic rules outlined in Chapter 4, it offers a good starting point for any newcomer to the game. It may also be your preferred choice if you intend to play more at home than in the casino.

The game starts with the dealer placing a chip per player in the pot as an ante (see page 135). He then deals five cards, face down, to each player. Once all of the players have looked at their cards the game moves on and the first betting interval starts (see page 56). Play begins with the first player to the dealer's left, who has the opportunity to call, raise or fold. Each player takes his turn and, once all bets on the table are equal, the draw takes place.

The draw
In the draw, each player left in the game, including the dealer, has the opportunity to discard a maximum of three cards in return for new ones. Starting with the first player to his left, the dealer hands out the cards to each one in turn and places the discards, face down, in a separate pile. Any player wishing to keep his five original cards is said to "stand pat" and indicates this by tapping the table or saying "None."

When the draw is over, a second betting interval takes place, again, with the first player to the dealer's left. Once more, each player has the option of calling, raising or folding in turn until all bets on the table are equal.

The showdown
The second betting interval is followed by the showdown. Starting with the last player to raise, each player states his hand. The player with the highest-ranking hand (see pages 52–53) wins and takes the pot.

Strategy
Although the game sounds simple, it can be very complex and repeated success depends on adopting **basic strategy** before the draw and understanding how many cards to draw in order to improve your hand. Many books have been written on the subject and readers are advised to carry our further reading before playing with significant sums of money.

Checking

During either betting interval, each player can check and may do so only until no bets have been placed, after which players must call, raise or fold. If, at the end of the first betting interval, all players have checked, the cards are returned to the dealer, reshuffled and dealt by the next dealer, who puts another chip per player in the pot – so doubling the ante for that deal.

Glossary

American wheel In roulette, a game using a wheel that has slots for both 0 and 00.

Ante In poker, a compulsory stake placed in the *pot* before a deal.

Back door In Texas hold'em or Omaha poker, to complete a flush or straight with the last two *board* cards when this was not a primary objective.

Banker In baccarat, the better whose role it is to deal the cards to himself and the *players*. The role passes to the right with each hand.

Betting interval In poker, the period in a deal where each player must fold, call, raise, or check. The number of betting intervals can vary, depending on the game being played.

Betting round In poker, the period in a *betting interval* in which each player folds, calls, raises, or checks in turn. There may be a number of betting rounds before the bets of all players still in the game are equal, and the *betting interval* ends.

Blackjack In blackjack, a two-card hand that totals 21, comprising an Ace and a 10-count card. Also known as a *natural*.

Black/red bet In roulette, a bet that the winning bet will be black or red.

Blind bet A compulsory bet made before the deal in poker. It differs from the *ante* in being an active bet – that is, it counts towards the better's total stake.

Bluff In poker, to mislead the other players in the game regarding the value of your hand.

Board The set of *community cards* on the table in Texas hold'em or Omaha poker.

Boxman In craps, the casino representative who supervises the game.

Burn To remove the top card from the pack before play to prevent cheating.

Bust In blackjack, to reach a total of more than 21.

Call In poker, to match the previous bet.

Caller In baccarat, the casino member who announces the results of the hands.

Cardsharp A professional gambler who cheats to win.

Case card In poker, the fourth card of a rank, when the other three are in play.

Cash in To exchange one's *chips* for cash and retire from the game.

Check To stay in a game of poker without adding to one's total stake. This is only possible while no other players place a bet during any one *betting interval*.

Chips Counters of various colors used to bet with. Each color represents a different monetary value (see box, page 12).

Clocking the wheel In roulette, tracking the results of a number of spins to see if any numbers or groups of numbers are spun more often than others.

Cocked dice In craps, one or more dice not lying flat on the table after a throw.

Column bet In roulette, a bet on any number within one of the three vertical columns on the betting layout.

Come-out roll In craps, the first roll of the dice by a new *shooter*, determining the shooter's point.

Community cards Those cards in games, such as Texas hold'em or Omaha poker, that are common to all players' hands.

Corner bet In roulette, a bet covering 0, 00, 1, 2, 3 on the betting layout.

Crap out In craps, to throw a 2, 3, or 12 on the *come-out roll*.

Craps In craps, any dice roll that shows a 2, 3, or 12.

Deuce A card of the 2 rank.

Do bet In craps, any bet that favors the *shooter* over the house. Also known as right betting.

Don't bet In craps, any bet that favors the house over the *shooter*. Also known as wrong betting.

Double down In blackjack, an option to make a second bet on the two-card hand by taking one more card.

Double-zero game In roulette, the game played in the US where the wheel has a pocket for both 0 and 00.

Dozen bet In roulette, a bet that the winning bet will be either in the first twelve (1 to 12), the second twelve (13 to 24) or the third twelve (25 to 36) numbers on the wheel.

Draw In draw poker, the exchange of some cards in a hand for others.

En prison In roulette, an option in the *single-zero* game in which an even-money bet is held for the next roll, rather than lost, if the ball lands in the 0 pocket.

Fifth street See *River*.

Five-number bet In roulette, a bet on any four numbers forming a block on the betting layout.

Flop In Texas hold'em or Omaha poker, the first three *community cards*.

Flush In poker, five cards of the same suit.

Fold To give up one's hand to the dealer and drop out of a deal.

Fourth street See *Turn*.

Full house In poker, a hand with three cards of the same rank and two of another.

Hard hand In blackjack, a hand where the Ace counts as one.

High/low bet In roulette, a bet that the winning bet will be either in the low numbers (1 to 18) or the high numbers (19 to 36).

Hit In blackjack, an option to receive an additional card.

Hole card A concealed card, dealt face down to the dealer in blackjack and variously to players in different versions of poker.

House edge The mathematical advantage that the casino has on every game, given as a percentage.

Insurance In blackjack, a separate bet in which a player bets that the dealer has a *blackjack*, made when the dealer's up card is an Ace.

Kicker In Texas hold'em or Omaha poker, the lower of the two hole cards each player holds.

Limits The minimum or maximum number of *chips* a player is allowed to bet.

Line bet In roulette, a bet on any two "streets" on the betting layout.

Loose player In poker, a player who bets in defiance of the odds.

Martingale system A negative-progression system of betting, where the better doubles his bet every time he loses.

Natural In baccarat, a point of 8 or 9; in blackjack, a point of 21 with two cards, an Ace and a 10-count; in craps, a 7 or 11 on the *come-out* roll.

No-limit In poker, a game in which players can bet as many *chips* as they currently have on the table.

Notional dealer In poker, the player – indicated by a disc or button that rotates around the table – who would be dealer for any given round in the absence of the casino dealer.

Nuts In Texas hold 'em and Omaha poker, the best possible hand in the game, taking into account the player's *hole cards* and the five *community cards*.

Odd/even bet In roulette, a bet that the winning bet will be odd or even.

On the button In poker, the *notional dealer* for any deal is said to be "on the button."

Paroli system A positive-progression system of betting, where the better doubles his bet every time he wins.

Pat hand In draw poker, a hand to which no cards are drawn.

Player In baccarat, the better who plays out the first hand in the game – usually the person with the highest bet on the Player hand winning.

Point In baccarat, the pip count of the two cards dealt to each player – always totalling

9 or less; in craps, a throw of 4, 5, 6, 8, 9, or 10 by the *shooter* on the *come-out roll* and which he must then throw a second time before throwing a 7.

Pot In poker, the *chips* at stake on the table.

Pot limit In poker, a game in which the maximum raise is the total in the *pot* at the time of betting.

Raise In poker, to call and increase the previous bet.

River In Texas hold'em or Omaha poker, the fifth and final community card. Also known as the fifth street.

Royal flush The highest hand in poker – A, K, Q, J, 10 of the same suit.

Seven out In craps, the point at which a *shooter* loses by throwing a 7 before repeating his *point*.

Shoe The box that holds the cards in various games.

Shooter In craps, the player whose turn it is to roll the dice.

Showdown In poker, the display of hands at the end of the game to determine the winner.

Side pot In poker, a separate *pot* contested by the other players when one player has *tapped out*.

Single-zero game In roulette, the game played in Europe where the roulette wheel has a single 0 pocket.

Soft hand In blackjack, a hand where the Ace counts as eleven.

Split In blackjack, the option to take another card to each of the two original cards when a player has been dealt a pair.

Split bet In roulette, a bet on any two adjoining numbers on the betting layout.

Stand In blackjack, the decision not to take any additional cards.

Stand pat In draw poker, to decline the exchange of cards at the draw.

Stickman In craps, the dealer whose role it is to call out the rolls, take any proposition bets, and to move the dice around the table using a stick.

Straight In poker, five unsuited cards of consecutive rank.

Straight bet In roulette, a bet on any single number on the wheel.

Straight flush In poker, five cards of consecutive rank and of the same suit.

Street bet In roulette, a bet on any three numbers in a row on the betting layout.

Suited If a player's two *hole cards* are of the same suit, they are said to be suited.

Supercasino A new breed of casino, emerging in Las Vegas in the early 1990s, that is vast in scale, with thousands of hotel rooms and all manner of side attractions, besides gambling.

Surrender In blackjack, the option to fold before taking any more cards, where the player forfeits half his bet.

Table stakes In poker, a game in which the player's bet is limited to the number of *chips* he has on the table.

Tap out In poker, a procedure that is forced on a player during a *betting interval* when he is unable to continue because he has insufficient *chips* to call the bet.

Tell In poker, a subconscious signal that lets other players know the strength of your hand.

Tie In blackjack, the result of a hand where both the banker and the player have the same point value. Betters with a stake on either hand retain their bets.

Tight player In poker, a player who bets only on a strong hand.

Tote board In roulette, an illuminated board above the table that displays the last 20 or so winning numbers.

Turn In Texas hold'em and Omaha poker, the fourth *community card* on the board. Also known as fourth street.

Up card Any card that is dealt face up.

Wild card In poker, a card that, by prior agreement, can represent any other card in the pack.

Index

Acknowledgments

Executive Editor Trevor Davies
Editor Jessica Cowie
Executive Art Editor Geoff Fennell
Design Lovelock & Co
Illustrations Sudden Impact Media
Senior Production Controller Martin Croshaw